# AROUND san francisco WITH KIDS

## by Clark Norton

Fodor's Travel Publications
New York • Toronto • London • Sydney • Auckland

www.fodors.com

**CREDITS**
**Writer:** Clark Norton

**Series Editors:** Karen Cure, Caroline Haberfeld
**Editor:** Andrea Lehman
**Editorial Production:** Nicole Revere
**Production/Manufacturing:** Robert Shields

**Design:** Fabrizio La Rocca, *creative director*;
Tigist Getachew, *art director*
**Illustration and Series Design:** Rico Lins, Keren Ora
Admoni/Rico Lins Studio

**ABOUT THE WRITER**
Clark Norton, author of *Fodor's Where Should We Take the Kids?: California,* writes about family travel for *Family Fun, Parenting,* and the *San Francisco Examiner*. He has two children.

**Fodor's Around San Francisco with Kids**

First Edition
ISBN 0-679-00491-2
ISSN 1526-1395

**Important Tip**
Although all prices, opening times, and other details in this book are based on information supplied to us at press time, changes occur all the time in the travel world, and Fodor's cannot accept responsibility for facts that become outdated or for inadvertent errors or omissions. So always confirm information when it matters, especially if you're making a detour to visit a specific place.

**Special Sales**
Fodor's Travel Publications are available at special discounts for bulk purchases for sales promotions or premiums. Special editions, including personalized covers, excerpts of existing guides, and corporate imprints, can be created in large quantities for special needs. For more information, contact your local bookseller or Special Markets, Fodor's Travel Publications, 201 East 50th Street, New York, NY 10022. Inquiries from Canada should be directed to your local Canadian bookseller or sent to Random House of Canada, Ltd., Marketing Dept., 2775 Matheson Boulevard East, Mississauga, Ontario L4W 4P7. Inquiries from the United Kingdom should be sent to Fodor's Travel Publications, 20 Vauxhall Bridge Road, London, England SW1V 2SA.

PRINTED IN THE UNITED STATES OF AMERICA
10 9 8 7 6 5 4 3 2 1

# CONTENTS

# WELCOME TO GREAT DAYS!

**B**etween pick-ups, drop-offs, and after-school activities, organizing a family's schedule is one full-time job. Planning for some fun time together shouldn't be another. That's where this book helps out. In creating it, our parent-experts have done all the legwork, so you don't have to. Open to any page and you'll find a great day together already planned out. You can read about the main event, check our age-appropriateness ratings to make sure it's right for your family, pick up some smart tips, and find out where to grab a bite nearby.

## HOW TO SAVE MONEY

Taking a whole family on an outing can be pricey, but there are ways to save.

**1.** Always ask about discounts at ticket booths. We list admission prices only for adults and kids, but an affiliation (and your ID) may get you a break. If you want to support a specific institution, consider buying a family membership up front. Usually these pay for themselves after a couple of visits, and sometimes they come with other good perks—gift-shop and parking discounts, and so on.

**2.** Keep an eye peeled for coupons. They'll save you $2 or $3 a head and you can find them everywhere from the supermarket to your pediatrician's office. Combination tickets, sometimes offered by groups of attractions, cost less than if you pay each admission individually.

**3.** Try to go on free days. Some attractions let you in at no charge one day a month or one day a week after a certain time.

## GOOD TIMING

Most attractions with kid appeal are busy when school is out. Field-trip destinations are sometimes swamped on school days, but these groups tend to leave by early afternoon, so weekdays after 2 during the school year can be an excellent time to visit museums, zoos, and aquariums. Outdoors, consider going after a rain—there's nothing like a downpour to clear away crowds. If you go on a holiday, call ahead—we list only the usual operating hours.

## SAFETY CATCH

Take a few sensible precautions. Show your kids how to recognize staff or security people when you arrive. And designate a meeting time and place—some visible landmark—in case you become separated. It goes without saying that you should keep a close eye on your children at all times, especially if they are small.

## FINAL THOUGHTS

We'd love to hear yours: What did you and your kids think about the places we recommend? Have you found other places we should include? Send us your ideas via e-mail (c/o editors@fodors.com, specifying the name of this book on the subject line) or snail mail (c/o Around San Francisco with Kids, Fodor's Travel Publications, 201 East 50th Street, New York, NY 10022). In the meantime, have a great day around San Francisco with your kids!

**THE EDITORS**

# ALCATRAZ ISLAND

The maximum-security prison on Alcatraz, closed in 1963, once held some of the nation's most incorrigible criminals—and though it's just 1¼ miles and a 10-minute boat ride from Fisherman's Wharf, the 12-acre island still seems eerily isolated, its lighthouse tower often shrouded in mist. Over the past 150 years, the Rock has been a fortification, military prison, federal penitentiary, and site of an American Indian occupation. But since becoming a national park in 1973, Alcatraz (from the Spanish word for "pelican") has also become one of San Francisco's most popular tourist sites. Its reputation as "America's Devil's Island" and its gorgeous views are irresistible lures.

Hop one of the Blue & Gold Fleet ferries, the only public transport to the island. Once here, you and your kids can peer into the tiny, spartan cells that once held the likes of Al Capone, Machine Gun Kelly, and Robert ("Birdman of Alcatraz") Stroud, and visit the grim "dark holes" where disobedient prisoners were left to languish by themselves in total darkness. Other sights include the mess hall (complete with the last day's menu), the library, and the exercise yard,

*HEY, KIDS!* Can you imagine sharks circling Alcatraz? That's what prison wardens and guards told inmates to scare them out of trying to escape. Actually, there were—and are—no sharks. In 1962, three prisoners did tunnel out with sharpened spoons. Though they made it off the island, they weren't seen again, so no one knows if they reached shore alive. This tale became the basis of *Escape From Alcatraz,* one of several films set here, including the more recent *The Rock.*

where catwalks and guard towers loomed overhead. From the concrete bleachers, prisoners could glimpse the gleaming city across the bay and smell the coffee roasting in North Beach. Surprisingly, although Alcatraz could hold 450 prisoners, no more than 250 were ever incarcerated at a time, and barely a tenth that number were here at the end.

Choose between taking a self-guided tour, using an audiocassette or pamphlet, or going with a ranger. (Most school-age kids love the riveting Cell House Audio Tour, which includes ex-inmates and guards describing their experiences.) When it's open—usually September–January, depending on bird-nesting season—the Agave Trail, along the island's southern rim, provides knockout views of city and bay. Tide pools line the water's edge, and a 110-step stone staircase leads to the old prison parade ground, now colonized by herons, gulls, and other wildlife. Allow about 2½ hours total for a visit.

KID-FRIENDLY EATS You can picnic around the Alcatraz dock but not beyond. The **Alcatraz Café and Grill** (Pier 39, tel. 415/434–1818), which serves burgers, pizza, and seafood, has a tiny cell and other prison themes. At the **Eagle Café** (Pier 39, tel. 415/433–3689), load up on big breakfasts and lunches in an old-time waterfront atmosphere.

KEEP IN MIND When planning a visit to Alcatraz, start early and dress appropriately. With only 300 people per sailing, advance boat reservations are strongly advised and are essential in summer or on holiday weekends throughout the year. Call or stop by the Pier 41 ticket window at least two weeks ahead. Bring some warm clothing, since the island and boat ride are often windy and chilly, and wear comfortable shoes for climbing over rocky and sometimes steep terrain.

# ANGEL ISLAND STATE PARK

Want to escape with your kids to an island park where the air is fresh, cars are banned, and grassy picnic areas, rocky coves, forested slopes, and 13 miles of hiking and biking trails await? Angel Island, the largest island in San Francisco Bay, is just a 40-minute ferry ride from the city.

The fun begins on the Blue & Gold Fleet ferry ride across the bay. Once on the island, you can spread out a blanket or grab a picnic table at Ayala Cove, not far from the ferry dock, where there's plenty of grass, shade, and a small beach. (Waters are cold and often rough and not meant for swimming; there are no lifeguards.) Lots of families hang out at the cove all day, tossing Frisbees or footballs.

Alternatively, you can set off on hiking or biking trips. The easiest route is the paved-and-gravel, mostly level 5-mile Perimeter Road, which rings the entire island and offers 360° views of the bay. Figure about 2½ hours to walk it. If that's too much, a one-hour narrated

## HEY, KIDS!

If you go hiking, keep an eye out for animals, such as deer and raccoons. You might also see birds, such as hawks, hummingbirds, blue herons, owls, pelicans, and grebes. And when you look out toward the water, watch for sea lions or harbor seals, which sometimes hang out just offshore.

## KEEP IN MIND
There are a number of ways to make a trip to Angel Island more pleasant, including choosing a good time to go. May and September tend to be less foggy—and less congested—than the summer months. Ferry and other services are limited from November to April. Dress in layers; the boat ride can get chilly. If bringing a bike, get to the ferry early; bike passage is limited and first-come, first-served. And unless you want to make an unexpected camping trip, allow plenty of time to catch the last ferry back to San Francisco.

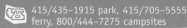 Departures: Pier 41, Fisherman's Wharf

 Park daily 8–sunset (except camping).
Ferry May–Oct, daily; Nov–Apr, Sa–Su

415/435–1915 park, 415/705–5555
ferry, 800/444–7275 campsites

 $11 adults, $10 youths
12–18, $6 children 5–11

3 and up

tram tour ($7–$10) covers much of the territory. If you like to bike, you can either bring your own or, from spring to fall, rent one near the dock ($10 per hour, $25 per day). Hikers can also climb to the top of the island on fairly narrow and steep dirt trails, recommended for kids 8 and older.

Older children might also enjoy sampling a bit of Angel Island's history. Once known as the "Ellis Island of the West," the island processed thousands of Chinese immigrants from 1910 to 1940. You can visit the long-abandoned barracks where many were detained for months or years. Old military installations and gun mounts, dating back to the Civil War, are also on view.

The island has nine hike-in campsites ($7–$11). Sites one–four are best for small groups. Bring charcoal or camp stove and prepare to haul equipment for 1 or 2 miles.

**KID-FRIENDLY EATS** Many families bring a picnic lunch. The **Cove Café** (tel. 415/897–0715), near the ferry dock on the island, serves sandwiches, salads, and soups on a harbor-view deck; the café is open March to November (March, April, and November limited days only). For restaurants near Pier 41, *see* Alcatraz Island, Fisherman's Wharf, and Pier 39.

# ARDENWOOD HISTORIC FARM

When was the last time your children got to pump water, crank an old clothes wringer, or plant some crops? If the only hands-on activity they've gotten lately is hitting the button on the remote control, then head for the antidote for urban couch potatodom: Ardenwood Historic Farm. Located in southern Alameda County and part of the East Bay Regional Park District, Ardenwood is the place to introduce city children to life on a real working farm—and a 19th-century farm at that. At this 200-acre complex, kids—and parents—can join in the pumping and cranking that were required to keep a farm going back in the Victorian age, and even help feed the livestock and plant, tend, and harvest the crops.

In addition, costumed docents give farm-chore and craft-making demonstrations, such as horseshoe hammering, hay harvesting, lace-making, barrel-making, and biscuit baking. As on any farm, the activities change from season to season and even week to week; what you see and do in spring will be quite different from in the fall.

**HEY, KIDS!** Besides learning about what people did on an old-time farm, you can see farmyard animals—sheep, goats, pigs, chickens, bunnies, turkeys, horses, and cows—and go on horse-drawn hay wagon and horse-drawn train rides, too. Mom and Dad should be happy to hear they won't have to pay any extra for these; they're included in the admission price.

 34600 Ardenwood Blvd., Fremont

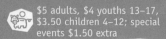 $5 adults, $4 youths 13–17, $3.50 children 4–12; special events $1.50 extra

 Apr–mid-Nov, Th–Su 10–5 (last entrance at 4); early Dec Christmas tours

510/796–0663 recording, 510/796–0199 voice

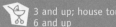 3 and up; house tour 6 and up

Ardenwood dates from the days following the 1849 Gold Rush, when a failed gold prospector named George Washington Patterson established a ranch here. Patterson's restored farmhouse and Victorian gardens are still on view, and you can take free tours of the house on a first-come, first-served basis.

Ardenwood also hosts a number of special events: old-fashioned Fourth of July and Christmas celebrations, summer and fall harvest festivals, concerts, and re-creations of Victorian-era social occasions. From late May through October, you can bring a little bit of Ardenwood home: Fresh-picked organic vegetables and flowers are on sale near the main gate. And after visiting this living yet historical farm, your children might just realize that potatoes don't grow on couches.

**KID-FRIENDLY EATS** Ardenwood has nice picnic areas (the grounds are also open Tuesdays and Wednesdays for picnics only) and the **Farmyard Café** (tel. 510/797–5621), selling hot dogs, ice cream, and, for special events, barbecued foods. Nearby restaurants include an **International House of Pancakes** (5687 Jarvis Ave., Newark, tel. 510/794–5687).

**KEEP IN MIND** To maintain the 19th-century atmosphere, Ardenwood doesn't allow anyone to bring modern play equipment onto the grounds. This includes electronic games and any contemporary sporting equipment, such as Frisbees, footballs, and soccer balls. Adult "toys" (cameras, video cameras, cell phones, and the like) are okay—but to get into the spirit of things, you may want to turn your beeper off. Despite their existence during the 19th century, dogs are not permitted.

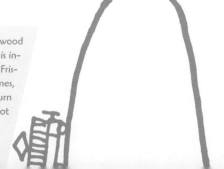

# BASIC BROWN BEAR FACTORY

**65**

The Basic Brown Bear Factory puts a new twist on shopping. At this Potrero Hill factory—one of the country's few remaining manufacturers of stuffed animals—your kids can choose from a wide range of styles and then help assemble and stuff their own teddy bears.

Here's how it works: Basic Brown Bear provides the pattern, material, stuffing, and instructions for a cuddly toy. Your child helps put it together, deciding how chubby or slender it will be, with staff and stuffing machine there to assist, too. A staff member then sews up the bear and grooms it, and your youngster provides the final touch with a blow-dry "bath." All you have to do is pay for it.

The cost of the teddy bears depends on the size and complexity of the patterns, all of which are made right at the factory. The least expensive (and simplest pattern), Baby Bear, stands 13 inches high and is priced at less than a dollar per inch. The most expensive, Giant PaPa Bear, stands 6 feet tall and costs nearly $1,000. Another pricey (but considerably more

## HEY, KIDS!

Here's the 411 on the factory: It was started in 1976 by Merrilee and Eric Woods, who made the first bear for their oldest son, then 3 years old. They got the idea to let kids stuff bears in 1985. Merrilee designs the bears—more than 30 models—and more than 40 outfits.

**KEEP IN MIND** Although you can take the tour or just watch the activity for free, the lure of making your own bear (not to mention the fear of disappointing your child) is so great that few families emerge bear naked. If you don't want to shell out the big bucks, consider calling for a catalogue before you visit, so that you can pre-select an appropriately priced bear. Depending on where you are, you might prefer to visit a mini-branch of Basic Brown Bear Factory at the Cannery (see the Cannery and Ghirardelli Square), but tours aren't given at this bear outpost.

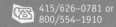

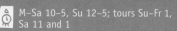

affordable) model, the California Bear, stands on all fours like the grizzly on the state flag, has soft velveteen claws, and runs 29 inches nose to tail. Two popular moderately priced models are known as the Basic Brown Bear (18 inches high) and his little sister, Gigi (15 inches high). The smallest bears with movable arms, legs, and heads are known as Stanley and Jeanette. In addition, a full range of accessories—dresses, tutus, jumpers, T-shirts, tuxedos, bridal outfits, vests, pants, surfer shirts, overalls, sleep shirts, sweaters, engineer outfits, and Nutcracker uniforms—are for sale.

The factory also gives free drop-in tours (geared for families or groups of 8 or fewer), on which you can see how the bears are designed, cut, and sewn. When all is said, done, and stuffed, your children will probably treasure these cuddly animals above others because they helped make them.z

**KID-FRIENDLY EATS** **San Francisco BBQ** (1328 18th St., tel. 415/431–8956) serves reasonably priced Thai barbecue (grilled chicken or beef) and noodle dishes in casual surroundings. **Sally's** (300 De Haro St., tel. 415/626–6006) is a breakfast-and-lunch spot known throughout the city for great omelets, home fries, and baked goods like scones and muffins.

# BAY AREA DISCOVERY MUSEUM

As any student of recent lingo and acronyms can attest, this is one BAD Museum. One of the state's top children's museums, it has a bonus: knockout views from its location virtually beneath the north end of the Golden Gate Bridge. The museum is housed in seven buildings that were once part of Ft. Baker, a military installation that guarded San Francisco Bay. It's now part of Golden Gate National Recreation Area, making this the nation's only children's museum in a national park. Of course, your kids will probably like the view okay, but it'll take second place to what happens inside. There children engage in all sorts of hands-on learning, which to the uninitiated bears a striking resemblance to playing.

Appropriately, the bay's natural wonders provide one realm of discovery. In the Bay Hall, your kids can crawl through a tunnel "beneath" the sea or fish aboard their own Discovery Boat. In the Maze of Illusions, mirrors and holograms challenge perception of color, dimension, and distance. Other attractions include an interactive Media Center, where youngsters check out computer animation; a science lab focusing on local plants and animals; art and ceramics

**HEY, KIDS!** If you can read this (and probably even if you can't), you're old enough for ceramics labs, given Saturdays 1:30–4:30 for kids 3 and up. Here you work with clay, perhaps making a pot, a figurine, or a treasure box, which the teacher will fire in a kiln (a type of oven). Come back another Saturday to glaze it and eventually take it home. You don't need to sign up in advance, but there is a $5 materials fee.

 Ft. Baker, 557 E. McReynolds Rd.,
Sausalito

 415/487–4398 recording,
415/289–7268 voice

$7 adults, $6 children
1–18; programs extra

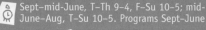 Sept–mid-June, T–Th 9–4, F–Su 10–5; mid-
June–Aug, T–Su 10–5. Programs Sept–June

 0–10

studios; and an architecture and design area. Toddlers have their own interactive discovery area—Tot Spot—where they can enter a storybook cave with adjustable lighting and an echo chamber, or sit on a waterbed and watch live fish above. Special exhibits change every few months.

Half-hour weekday morning drop-in programs cater to toddlers and preschoolers. Kids in Jumping Jelly Beans learn storytelling through creative movement; those taking Bangin', Twangin' and Shakin' sing, dance, and play instruments. Smoosh and Squish comprises three art workshops (ceramics, painting, and collage). And if you haven't quite gotten your fill here, the museum's Discovery Store stocks educational and entertaining books, CD-ROMs, activity kits, and art supplies to take home.

### KEEP IN MIND
Almost all exhibits are indoors, but outside in a play area called Discovery Park, bridges, trucks, and boats await. So if it's rainy or cold, bring appropriate clothing. Even if your child won't be playing in Discovery Park, you have to walk some between buildings. Besides, you'll want to pause on your way home to admire the views.

**KID-FRIENDLY EATS** The museum's **Discovery Café** (tel. 415/289–7269) has indoor and outdoor seating and foods appealing to both kids (hot dogs, burgers, peanut butter and jelly sandwiches) and parents (sandwiches and salads with ingredients like goat cheese and sun-dried tomatoes). You can also picnic on the grounds. If you want to eat in downtown Sausalito, the creatively named **Hamburgers** (737 Bridgeway, tel. 415/332–9471) has, you guessed it, burgers and fries for takeout until 5. You can also sit inside, though it's cramped.

# BAY CRUISES

A big part of the San Francisco Bay experience is getting out on the water—and kids are usually among the most enthusiastic boat riders. Two of the most popular trips go to Alcatraz Island and Angel Island State Park (*see above*), and, May–October, you can even combine them in a one-day extravaganza offered by the Blue & Gold Fleet. But there are plenty of other options if you just want a boat trip without touring islands on the other end.

One-hour narrated bay cruises hit the highlights, passing by Alcatraz and under the Golden Gate Bridge. Take your pick between the Blue & Gold Fleet, operating from Pier 39's West Marina, and the Red & White Fleet, leaving from Pier 43½ at Fisherman's Wharf. The cost is the same, but note that the Blue & Gold cruise is part of CityPass (*see* the California Academy of Sciences).

There's no narration on Golden Gate Ferry boats, departing from the Ferry Building (the Embarcadero and Market St.) for Sausalito, a Mediterranean-style seaside village in Marin County. However, the scenery's as good and prices are much lower; there are even Weekend

## HEY, KIDS!

If you take a Hornblower Dining Yachts cruise, ask a crew member if you can visit the wheelhouse. You'll be glad you did. You can talk with the captain and watch him sail the yacht, and he can answer your questions—like just how fast can a dining yacht go?

**KEEP IN MIND** Even on the bay, which is usually placid compared to the ocean, you might want to take seasickness precautions for your children (check with your pediatrician on appropriate medications). Also remember that it can get very cold and windy on the water, even on a sunny day; dress in layers.

Boats leave from Fisherman's Wharf,
the Ferry Building, and Sausalito

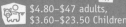 Blue & Gold: 415/773-1188; Red & White: 415/447-0597;
Golden Gate: 415/923-2000; *Hawaiian Chieftain*: 415/331-
3214; Hornblower: 415/788-8866

 $4.80–$47 adults,
$3.60–$23.50 Children

 Daily with varying times

5 and up

Family Fares. Blue & Gold Fleet runs ferries to Sausalito, as well as to Tiburon (North Bay), Muir Woods (*see below*) via Tiburon, and, in the East Bay, to Alameda/Oakland and Vallejo—the latter home of Six Flags Marine World (*see below*).

The tall ship *Hawaiian Chieftain* (3020 Bridgeway, Suite 266, Sausalito), a striking replica of an 18th-century trading vessel, sails the bay April–October. (In winter, it sails along the California coast and in the Sacramento Delta.) On four-hour Saturday Adventure Sails (reservations required), your family can lend a hand with the lines and then recharge with a buffet lunch on board. The boat leaves from Sausalito's Marina Plaza Harbor, off Marinship Way.

Hornblower Dining Yachts (Pier 33) offers weekday lunch and weekend brunch cruises, serving bountiful meals aboard elegant boats. These trips are best for children 8 or older. For all trips, it's best to call for schedules and prices.

**KID-FRIENDLY EATS** The *Hawaiian Chieftain* and Hornblower Dining Yachts both include large buffet meals in their rates. For restaurants in the Fisherman's Wharf area, *see* Alcatraz Island, Fisherman's Wharf, and Pier 39. For restaurants near the Ferry Building, *see* the International Children's Art Museum and Embarcadero Center.

# BAY MODEL VISITOR CENTER

**62**

Everyone knows San Francisco is the City by the Bay, but the size and geography of the bay—as well as other nearby waterways and the vast Sacramento Delta—can be confusing even for longtime residents. This 1½-acre hydraulic three-dimensional scale model of the bay housed inside a onetime shipbuilding facility helps you make sense of all that water.

Operated by the U.S. Army Corps of Engineers, the Bay Model looks like a cross between a science experiment and a huge work of modern art. Don't expect bells and whistles, though; this is a scientific facility. It was built in the 1950s to test possible ways of damming the bay to store fresh water. No dams were ever built, however, and the model now enables scientists and engineers to study the bay's water flow and tidal patterns and to measure the effects of both natural phenomena (such as drought and floods) and human activities on local waters. It's all intended to help the corps protect wetlands, control flooding, manage natural disasters, and keep waterways navigable.

**KEEP IN MIND** Tours of the Bay Model are self-guided, so pick up a map when you enter. If you have a minimum of 10 people in your group, however, you can reserve a ranger-led tour. Rangers will gear the presentation toward the ages of the kids and whatever your particular interests are, so round up another like-minded family or two if you can. Audiotape tours are also available, though younger kids might find these a bit boring. Allow about 1½ hours for any tour, all of which are free.

 2100 Bridgeway, Sausalito

415/332-3870 recording, 415/332-3871 voice

 Free

Memorial Day-Labor Day, T-F 9-4, Sa-Su 10-5; early Sept-late May, T-Sa 9-4

8 and up

For young visitors (fourth grade and up is best), hands-on educational exhibits and videos depict the bay's natural history, wildlife, geology, and fishing industry. You and your children can walk on ramps to get an overview of the bay's enormity. The model comprises nearly 300 12-foot by 12-foot, 5-ton slabs of concrete, representing 343 square miles of bay, river, ocean, and land, all reproduced to scale. The model encompasses the South Bay (down to San Jose), Central Bay (including San Francisco and Oakland), San Pablo Bay (Marin County), the Golden Gate, the narrows of the Carquinez Strait, Suisun Bay (California's largest remaining tidal wetland), and the delta's labyrinth of river channels, sloughs, and islands, from which freshwater flows into San Francisco Bay before mixing with saltwater and emptying into the Pacific. Though it's worth seeing at any time, the best time to come is when the model is operational and you can actually watch the tides flowing through the bay, so call ahead for schedules.

**HEY, KIDS!** Among the Bay Model's interactive exhibits is a debris-retrieval video game. Now don't roll your eyes; it's more fun than it sounds! You can also learn about the bay's geography and tides via touch screens.

**KID-FRIENDLY EATS** You can picnic on one of the benches in the grassy park areas between Bridgeway and the bay, near the ferry terminal. **Scoma's** (588 Bridgeway, tel. 415/332-9551) has bay views, decent seafood, and a children's menu. Also on Bridgeway is **Hamburgers** (*see* the Bay Area Discovery Museum), a takeout restaurant.

# BURLINGAME MUSEUM OF PEZ
## MEMORABILIA

Housed in a former computer store in the town of Burlingame, just south of San Francisco, this is the world's first and only museum devoted to Pez, the Austrian-made peppermint candy that comes in the plastic dispensers with the wacky flip-top heads. (Pez is short for *Pfefferminz,* the German word for peppermint.) Any child who likes collections or candy (or collecting candy) will get a kick out of the largest public display of Pez dispensers in the world. In the gift shop—bigger than the rest of the museum—your kids (or, more likely, you) can buy plenty of Pez or Pez collectibles, including Pez puzzles, posters, and T-shirts.

Children can look for dispensers with Disney characters—Mickey Mouse was the first ever, dating from the early 1950s—as well as Santa Claus, the Pink Panther, *Star Wars* characters, Smurfs, zoo animals, Batman, Kermit the Frog and Miss Piggy, the Ninja Turtles, Bugs Bunny, or the all-time best-seller, Winnie-the-Pooh. The museum also shows video clips of Pez appearances in movies—*ET, Stand By Me, The Client* (which featured an "Elvis Pezley")—and on TV (a Krusty Pez on *The Simpsons,* a Tweety Bird Pez on *Seinfeld*).

**KEEP IN MIND** Chances are you won't leave the museum without a Pezzy purchase—perhaps a Glowing Ghost Pez, Nintendo Pez, or Pez flashlight—but remember that the candy tastes as good from a $2 dispenser as from a $1,000 one. (Your kids might need to be reminded of that, too.)

**HEY, KIDS!** Look for the Golden Glow Pez dispenser (made from 1955 to 1965); it looks like real gold, but isn't. Pez guns, made from the 1950s until 1982, are another novelty, as are Body Parts Pez, which were made for just three years and are designed to fit over other Pez dispensers. (The skeleton Body Parts is a hit at Halloween.) But the rarest Pez of all is the Make-a-Face dispenser, made for only a few months in 1972.

214 California Dr., Burlingame

  Free

 T–F 10–6, Sa 10–5

650/347–2301

5 and up

The man behind the museum is Gary Doss, who sold computers here for 10 years until the Pez dispensers he started displaying for fun proved more popular than the PCs. Doss has now amassed a permanent collection of some 400 different dispensers; he's missing only seven from all those ever made. A display box of some 300 dispensers contains such rarities as Bicentennial Pez, Olympic Pez, Psychedelic Eye Pez (a giant hand with an eyeball in it, from 1968), and Arithmetic Pez, which sports a slide rule.

Don't get the idea that this is all penny-candy stuff, however. Countless people collect dispensers, and four Pez conventions are held each year around the country. One of Doss's most valuable pieces is a 1964-era Mary Poppins dispenser worth about $1,200. If only you'd kept that Popeye Pez from when you were little!

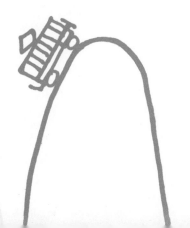

**KID-FRIENDLY EATS** **Christie's Restaurant** (245 California Dr., tel. 650/347–9440), which serves breakfast and lunch daily, is located right across from the museum. With a counter, a few outdoor tables, and a bustling atmosphere, it dishes up such staples as eggs, burgers, fries, and hot and cold sandwiches. For good Italian food in nice surroundings, and children's menus to boot, the local branch of **Il Fornaio** (327 Lorton Ave., tel. 650/375–8000) is always reliable.

# CABLE CAR MUSEUM

When a cable car comes by—bells clanging, brakes screeching, cables humming—everybody, whether kid or grown-up, turns to watch. Cable cars are the only National Historic Landmarks that *move*. But what is it that makes these Victorian-age conveyances go (without engines!) and keeps them on track—up and down some of the city's steepest hills? You'll find out at the Cable Car Museum.

Of course, first you have to get there, and the only way to go is by cable car. Well, you could drive—but what fun would that be? (And parking is nearly impossible to find anyway.) Hop on the Powell-Mason Line or the Powell-Hyde Line either downtown or in the Fisherman's Wharf area. Then ask the conductor to call out the Cable Car Museum, situated in the 1907 redbrick cable car barn and powerhouse at the corner of Washington and Mason streets, near Chinatown. The cable car ride costs $2 per person (under 5 free), but with free admission to the museum, you're still ahead of the game.

**HEY, KIDS!** When you take your cable car ride, be sure to keep an eye on the gripman and brakeman in action. The gripman works the lever that grips the cable beneath the street, making the car go forward. If he lets go, the car stops—with the help of the brakeman, who works the brakes. On steep hills and around curves, especially, the two men have to rely on teamwork, timing, and muscle.

1201 Mason St.

 415/474–1887

 Free

 Apr–Sept, daily 10–6; Oct–Mar, daily 10–5

3 and up

Once inside, you'll learn the ingenious secrets of cable power, developed more than 125 years ago by Andrew Hallidie, an engineer and immigrant from Scotland, who tested the first cable car on nearby Clay Street. It's simple, really: The four sets of cables make a continuous 9½-mph circuit beneath city streets; the cars, which grip the cables, automatically travel along with them. The cable system—on view on the lower level here—is run by huge revolving wheels that pull and steer the cables as they enter and leave the powerhouse. (You can hear the whirring sounds as soon as you come in.) Up on the mezzanine, there's a museum displaying three antique model cable cars, including the first one Hallidie built in 1873. You'll also find plenty of old photographs, a 16-minute film showing how cable cars operate, and a museum shop.

KID-FRIENDLY EATS The **Pot Sticker** (150 Waverly Pl., tel. 415/397–9985) is a good place to try inexpensive Chinese food, such as steamed or panfried dumplings filled with meat or vegetables. **Mo's Gourmet Hamburgers** (1322 Grant Ave., tel. 415/788–3779), in North Beach, serves up, you guessed it, a variety of big, juicy burgers in casual surroundings.

KEEP IN MIND Cable cars are often crowded, and long lines form at the turnarounds, where passengers gather to make sure of getting seats. But you don't have to board at turnarounds; cars stop every other block or so (look for maroon-and-white signs). If you board en route, approach the car quickly as it pauses, wedge into an available space, and hold on tight. (Make sure small children are safely inside, holding on, before the car moves.) You can pay on board or buy a ticket at one of the self-service machines at some terminals.

# CALIFORNIA ACADEMY OF SCIENCES

**59**

This huge complex in the heart of Golden Gate Park is actually three family attractions in one—a natural history museum, aquarium, and planetarium providing windows into the earth, ocean, and space.

Start with the Natural History Museum, one of the world's 10 largest. At the Earthquake exhibit, your children can experience simulated quakes, complete with special effects, so Californians can get psyched for the Big One and out-of-staters can see what the fuss is about. Wild California presents a lifelike re-creation—with sound effects—of birds and marine mammals on the rocky Farallon Islands. The Hall of Fossils displays dinosaur bones, including a brontosaurus skull. At the exotic African Safari hall, a water-hole diorama is so realistic, you may feel like drinking alongside the (stuffed) animals. You'll also find a gem and mineral hall, insect room, human cultures hall, the Far Side of Science cartoons gallery, and Early Childhood, an open play-learning space for small children.

## HEY, KIDS!

Be sure to visit the aquarium's incredibly cute black-footed penguins at feeding time—11:30 and 4. At the Fish Roundabout, where leopard sharks, sea bass, silver salmon, tuna, and pompano swim in a 100,000-gallon circular tank, you can watch the feeding frenzy daily at 2.

**KEEP IN MIND** One ticket covers both museum and aquarium. The planetarium costs extra, but you needn't pay museum admission to see Laserium. The Golden Gate Park Explorer Pass ($14 adults, kids free) includes admission to the Academy (excluding the planetarium), several other museums, and the Japanese Tea Garden; it is sold here, at many hotels, and at the Hallidie Plaza Visitors Center. CityPass ($27.75 adults, $17.25 youths 12–17, kids free) is good for nine days at the Academy, four other museums, the zoo, and a bay cruise.

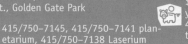
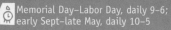
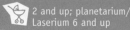
At the Steinhart Aquarium, kids can eyeball over 15,000 fresh- and saltwater fish and other aquatic creatures. Whether it's piranhas, manatees, jellyfish, sea horses, seals, dolphins, green sea turtles, eerie garden eels (who stick their heads menacingly out of sand), electric fish, slithery water monitors, alligator gars—fish that resemble gators—or real alligators lying still as logs, you can find them in some 165 tanks approximating natural habitats. At the Touch Tidepool, young ones can pick up sea stars, anemones, and slimy sea cucumbers. In the 600,000-gallon living tropical reef, they'll see reef sharks and brilliantly colored fish swimming around equally beautiful coral.

Reached through the museum, the Morrison Planetarium is Northern California's largest star show. Multimedia presentations reveal the night sky through the ages under a 55-foot dome, with music and such special effects as whirling through galaxies and entering black holes (potentially frightening for preschoolers). Laserium light shows are played to hour-long rock soundtracks, such as Pink Floyd's *Dark Side of the Moon*.

**KID–FRIENDLY EATS** The museum's **cafeteria** is open until an hour before closing. If you crave seafood after visiting the aquarium, head for nearby **PJ's Oysterbed** (737 Irving St., tel. 415/566–7775), serving Louisiana-style fish and shellfish in a festive atmosphere. **Pasta Pomodoro** (816 Irving St., tel. 415/566–0900), part of a mini-chain, produces good pastas for low prices, amid bustling, casual surroundings. **Park Chow** (1240 9th Ave., tel. 415/665– 9912) has good spaghetti and home-style pies.

# CALIFORNIA PALACE OF THE
## LEGION OF HONOR

One of the city's top fine-arts museums, the California Palace of the Legion of Honor is a showcase for European paintings, sculpture, tapestries, and furniture dating back to medieval times. Works by the French Impressionists and the sculptor Rodin are highlights. Equally stunning is the gleaming palace-like structure itself, which was designed in 1924 in the style of the 18th-century Palais de Legion d'Honneur in Paris and intended as a memorial to California's World War I dead. Renovated in the 1990s, with a pyramidal glass skylight illuminating the new lower-level galleries, the museum occupies a splendid location in Lincoln Park overlooking the Golden Gate. Rodin's famous sculpture *The Thinker,* made from an 1880 cast, sits just outside the front entrance.

Depending on the ages of your children, allow about an hour or two for a typical visit. Stick to the basics. Many school-age kids enjoy paintings by French Impressionists, and the museum has one of Monet's famous "Water Lilies." Be sure to take them to the two Rodin galleries, too, which contain about 70 works by the French sculptor (see if they can spot

**KEEP IN MIND** One of the bonuses of a trip to the museum is Lincoln Park, 270 acres of greenery atop a hillside in the Richmond District. At the eastern end of the park, 200-foot-high cliffs provide some of the city's best vantage points of the Golden Gate Bridge. The Lincoln Park Golf Course, a reasonably priced public course whose fairways are lined with towering Monterey cypress trees, is also here. Hiking trails, best suited for ages 6 and up, lead all the way from here to Land's End near the Cliff House (*see below*) via the rugged San Francisco Headlands.

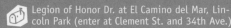 Legion of Honor Dr. at El Camino del Mar, Lincoln Park (enter at Clement St. and 34th Ave.)

 415/863–3330 recording, 415/750–3658 classes, 415/221–9911 golf

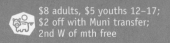 $8 adults, $5 youths 12–17; $2 off with Muni transfer; 2nd W of mth free

 T–Su 9:30–5

 3 and up

the one called *Man With a Broken Nose*). And if your kids haven't been exposed to much European art, they can see their first examples of Rubens and Rembrandt here.

On most Saturday afternoons, you can take part in one of the special one-hour programs the museum offers for kids and their parents. Kids aged 7–12 can attend Doing and Viewing Art, which includes gallery tours and art classes. Slightly smaller art aficionados (ages 3–6) get their own chance to see and try their hands at art in Big Kids, Little Kids (parental accompaniment required for this one). Just show up at 2; the programs are free with paid museum admission. But you'll want to call ahead to make sure the classes are offered the day you come.

**KID-FRIENDLY EATS** The museum's **Legion of Honor Cafe** (tel. 415/221–2233) offers Pacific views; weekend lunches are crowded, though. Local favorite **Bill's Place** (2315 Clement St., tel. 415/221–5262) serves juicy burgers and has patio dining. Families love **Ton Kiang**'s (5821 Geary Blvd., tel. 415/387–8273) outstanding Chinese food, so go early, especially on weekends.

**HEY, KIDS!** Think art museums are boring? The story behind this one isn't. It all started because of a rivalry between two wealthy San Francisco families. Millionaire Adolph Spreckels and his wife, Alma, financed the palace, at least partly, to show up the de Youngs, who had built a museum in Golden Gate Park. Adolph even shot and wounded M.H. de Young, publisher of the *San Francisco Chronicle*, which had printed stories critical of him. How's that for a real soap opera!

# THE CANNERY AND GHIRARDELLI SQUARE

These two family-friendly shopping complexes at Fisherman's Wharf, separated by one block, were pioneers in the concept of redeveloping decaying industrial sites as thriving urban commercial centers. Besides preserving a bit of local history and architecture, both offer attractions geared to families, exceptional bay views, and easy access via cable car.

The Cannery, a maze-like three-story brick structure dating from 1907, began as the world's largest peach-canning plant for what became the Del Monte Fruit and Vegetable Cannery. Until 1937, when the plant closed, tons of California fruits and vegetables were canned here for shipment worldwide. The Cannery was imaginatively renovated 30 years later and today has 45 specialty shops, restaurants, and galleries connected by walkways, archways, balconies, and bridges. In an olive-tree-lined courtyard, where you can snack on warm days, street performers often display their talents before passing the hat. A mini-branch of the Basic Brown Bear Factory (see above) is here, as is the free Museum of the City of San Francisco (tel. 415/928–0289). Open Wednesday–Sunday 10–4, it comprises an easy-to-browse-

## HEY, KIDS!

Ghirardelli Square holds a September chocolate lovers' festival. Sample truffles, brownies, and chocolate-covered wontons; decorate chocolate bars and shortcake; and watch a sundae-eating contest whose prize is the winner's weight in chocolate. (Makes you wish you were bigger, no?)

## KID-FRIENDLY EATS

At the Cannery, you can grab a snack (such as crepes and shish kebabs) from one of the **carts or cafés** in the courtyard and eat at a picnic table if the weather's nice. There are also several sit-down restaurants, some with outdoor tables. At Ghirardelli Square, **McCormick and Kuleto's Seafood Restaurant** (tel. 415/929–1730) has terrific bay views—and pretty good fish, too. The **Ghirardelli Chocolate Manufactory and Soda Fountain** (tel. 415/474–3938) is a must for dessert or a snack.

The Cannery, Leavenworth St., between Beach and Jefferson Sts.; Ghirardelli Square, 900 North Point St., at Larkin St.

Cannery June–Aug, Su–T 10–6:30, W–Sa 10–8:30; Sept–May, daily 10–6. Square daily 10–6, 9 in summer

 415/771–3112 the Cannery, 415/775–5500 Ghirardelli Square

Free; some attractions charge

5 and up

through collection of historic photos and artifacts from the 1906 earthquake, the Sutro Baths, San Francisco in the '60s, and other high and low points in the city's past.

To find Ghirardelli Square, look for the high clock tower and the huge electric sign, 25 feet high and 125 feet across. What started as a chocolate factory in 1893 and was owned for 60 years by the Ghirardelli family was transformed in 1964 into an open-air complex of some 50 specialty shops, cafés, and galleries. Retaining their original redbrick architecture, the buildings fill a city block. The square's most popular tenant, appropriately, is the Ghirardelli Chocolate Manufactory and Soda Fountain, where families come to gorge on huge sundaes, floats, and other chocolate concoctions. You can still watch chocolate being made in original vats and ovens in the old-fashioned ice cream parlor. As at the Cannery, street performers often take to the plaza stage to impress with feats of juggling and magic.

**TRANSPORTATION** The best, or at least most fun, way to get to either Ghirardelli Square or the Cannery is via the Powell-Hyde cable-car line, whose terminus is near the Hyde Street Pier, just a block or so from either shopping complex. Most kids love riding the cars down steep Hyde Street hill, with the bay and the historic ships at Hyde Street Pier straight ahead. The route passes by Union Square and Chinatown on its way to Fisherman's Wharf.

# CARTOON ART MUSEUM

This is the museum where Bill Watterson's classic comic duo, Calvin and Hobbes, live on. So do old-timers Krazy Kat and the Green Lantern. You'll also find the familiar figures of Snoopy, Charlie Brown, Batman, Bugs Bunny, and Dennis the Menace. Here, cartoons are treated with all the reverence usually accorded other types of art—hence the name, Cartoon Art Museum. Founded in 1984, it's the only museum on the West Coast that's dedicated to preserving, collecting, and exhibiting original cartoon art in all its forms.

The museum's 12,000-piece permanent collection displays works from 1730 (a William Hogarth drawing) to the present ("Peanuts," "Doonesbury," "Zippy the Pinhead" strips). Included in the collection, besides comic strips, are editorial and political cartoons, comic books (including underground and avant-garde), magazines, advertisements, newspapers, sculptures, and animation drawings. Among the latter, look for animation cels from Bugs Bunny cartoons, Pink Panther productions, and Peanuts TV shows as well as Disney studio drawings from such films as *Pinocchio, Fantasia, Snow White, Peter Pan,* and *101 Dalmatians.* Your kids may also

**HEY, KIDS!** If you're aged 8–14 and your parents are willing to invest in your budding art career, you can take cartooning classes here in the Children's Gallery. They're given by a professional cartoonist and teach you how to draw some of your favorite cartoon characters as well as how to design your own creations. Classes last 2½ hours and cost $35, with materials included; call the museum for times.

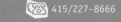 814 Mission St.

415/227–8666

$5 adults, $3 students,
$2 children 6–12

W–F 11–5, Sa 10–5, Su 1–5

 5 and up

enjoy discovering old-time comic strip artists like Jimmy Hatlo ("They'll Do It Every Time") and Harold Foster ("Prince Valiant").

Near Yerba Buena Gardens (*see below*), the museum occupies part of the second floor in an aging office building whose elevator can get a bit cranky. But thanks to 6,000 square feet of gallery space, the cartoon art on display is given plenty of room on uncrowded walls. One room is given over to temporary exhibitions, generally honoring a single artist or group of like-minded artists or strips. Another spotlights Bay Area artists. The museum has completed a Children's Gallery, in which kids can take how-to classes in drawing their own strips. Creation of a video and CD-ROM library is in progress.

## KID-FRIENDLY EATS
**Max's Diner** (311 3rd St., tel. 415/546–6297) serves huge sandwiches (try the juicy Reubens) but also has a kids' menu with bite-size burgers, among other choices. The biggest selection of nearby restaurants is at the **Metreon,** part of the Yerba Buena Gardens complex; *see* that listing for places to get sandwiches, salads, or Asian noodles.

## KEEP IN MIND
Two caveats: Some cartoons on display (especially in special exhibitions) may be R- or X-rated. If this is a concern, you may want to do a little advance scouting or call the museum first before bringing young kids. And be prepared to shell out some dough (or have your children bring their allowance money) for the inevitable moment when young eyes spy the gift shop. The store is filled with comic and cartoon books as well as mugs and T-shirts with cartoon characters on them.

# CHABOT OBSERVATORY AND
## SCIENCE CENTER

An observatory since 1883, and in its longtime location in the Oakland Hills since 1915, the Chabot Observatory and Science Center was slated at press time to move into a new $70 million, state-of-the-art facility a few miles away in Joaquin Miller Park (also in the Oakland Hills) by early 2000.

Spurred by fears of earthquake damage, the old observatory was made off limits to school classes (though not to the general public) in the 1970s. The new, higher-elevation (1,540 feet) observatory will enable schoolkids to resume astronomy classes there and allow everyone to have access to the country's largest telescope that's regularly open to the public—a 36-inch reflector. The observatory's historic 8-inch and 20-inch refractors are still on hand, too.

But kids and parents get much more besides a new observatory. Among the new attractions are a 275-seat planetarium, being billed as the most advanced in the world, and a large-screen, 225-seat domed Science Theater, similar to an OMNIMAX theater.

## HEY, KIDS!

The observatory's Junior Astronomers Club, a free organization for students grades 4 through 6, helps you learn about and find stars and planets in the sky, lets you look through the large telescopes, and see planetarium programs. Call (or have your parents call) the observatory for more information.

**KEEP IN MIND** The observatory sponsors a variety of classes for kids during the summer: Space Camp and Tech Camp for grades 6 to 8, Astronomy for Kids for grades 2 to 4, the Obedient Robot for girls in grades 6 to 9, and others. The observatory also offers weekend evening birthday parties, which include star-gazing sessions, weather permitting.

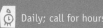 10902 Skyline Blvd., Oakland

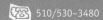 510/530-3480

 Call for prices

 Daily; call for hours

6 and up

Meanwhile, at the facility's innovative new science center, you'll find three exhibition halls with a variety of permanent and temporary hands-on exhibits that focus on astronomy and the interrelationships of all sciences and technology. There's also a Challenger Center, which has space-station and mission-control simulators; a Virtual Science Center multimedia and on-line education facility; laboratories; and classrooms. Outdoors, you'll find a hillside amphitheater and a 6-acre environmental education area and nature trail.

Since some details were still not settled at press time, why not visit the new facility and discover all it has to offer?

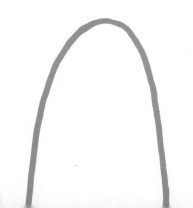

**KID-FRIENDLY EATS** The science center will have a **café** and tented **dining terrace** serving food to appeal to any age. Joaquin Miller Park has plenty of picnic space. For restaurants in Oakland's Lake Merritt area, *see* Children's Fairyland.

# CHILDREN'S FAIRYLAND

Before there was Disneyland, there was Children's Fairyland, which has enchanted small children from Oakland and throughout the Bay Area for a half century. In fact, this storybook theme park is said to have helped inspire the idea for Walt Disney's Magic Kingdom; Disney himself visited here a few years before opening his Anaheim theme park in 1955. There's even a "magic" connection here; a Magic Key, purchased for a one-time fee, unlocks "talking storybooks," bringing more than 30 colorful nursery rhyme and fairy-tale sets to life. You won't find any teens zooming by on daredevil rides or any high-tech gadgets catering to the over-10 set here. At this clean, low-key theme park, the stage is set entirely for young kids.

Your children can gaze through the window of Geppetto's workshop, pass through Alice in Wonderland's tunnel, enter the mouth of Willie the Whale, visit Peter Rabbit's Village, and view the Three Billy Goats Gruff—complete with live goats. Puppet shows, storytelling, a maze, slides, arts and crafts activities, and a little animal corral with a donkey, lamb, calves, and a horse provide more entertainment. So do a few gentle mini-rides—a carousel, a Ferris

**HEY, KIDS!** Children's Fairyland hosts a number of special events throughout the year, including a maypole dance in the spring and a Mad Hatter's Tea Party in the summer. But most kids' favorite is the Jack-O-Lantern Jamboree at Halloween, when sets and rides get taken over by ghosts, pirates, and other scary things. There's even trick-or-treating throughout the park, and usually there's no extra charge. Ask Mom or Dad to call for a schedule.

Grand and Bellevue Aves.,
Lakeside Park, Oakland

510/238-6876 recording,
510/452-2259 voice

$5 ages 1 and up,
Magic Key $1.65

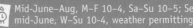
Mid-June–Aug, M–F 10–4, Sa–Su 10–5; Sept–
mid-June, W–Su 10–4, weather permitting

1–9

wheel, a boat ride, and a train—all of which are included in the new unlimited-ride admission price.

One of the newest additions to Children's Fairyland is called Play Island. Based on the tale of the Swiss Family Robinson, it's not a real island—more like a tree house with different levels—but kids do cross bridges to get there. There's lots of sand to play in, tropical-style huts with thatched roofs, and sound effects—listen for the bongo drums.

For safety reasons, no adults are admitted to Children's Fairyland without kids, or vice versa.

**KID-FRIENDLY EATS** There's plenty of grass and shade trees along the banks of Lake Merritt for spreading out a picnic blanket. **Zza's Trattoria** (552 Grand Ave., tel. 510/839–9124) is an informal, child-friendly Italian restaurant near the lake. **Zachary's Chicago Pizza** (5801 College Ave., tel. 510/655–6385) has some of the area's best deep-dish pies.

**KEEP IN MIND** No trip to Children's Fairyland is complete without time spent in the rest of 120-acre Lakeside Park, on pretty Lake Merritt. A natural saltwater lake—a rare phenomenon in the middle of a city—Lake Merritt was the country's first state game refuge, and there's still a waterfowl refuge here. Playgrounds, gardens, picnic spots, a natural science center, a bandstand, and waterfowl-feeding areas await at various points around the park. You can take a stroll around the lake or even a boat ride (see the Oakland Museum of California).

# CHINA BEACH

Pocket-size China Beach isn't a snap to find, but for those who seek it out, a reward awaits: It's one of the few beaches in San Francisco where it's generally gentle and safe enough to swim. Named for a group of poor Chinese fishermen who lived beside the beach during the Gold Rush era and now tucked below the palatial homes of the tony Seacliff area in the Richmond District, China Beach is a 600-foot sandy strip that's shielded by cliffs on either side. Its sheltered location heads off the treacherous waves that batter other, better-known city beaches, such as Ocean Beach (*see below*), and make swimming at those beaches so risky.

Not that China Beach is an entirely pleasant place to take a dip. The water tends to be pretty chilly, hovering around the 60s in summer, and, like all San Francisco beaches, it's subject to being socked in by summer fog. But if you can get past the teeth-chattering, it's a nice spot to bring swimming-age kids and let them wade off into the water without undue fears (note, however, that there are no longer lifeguards here). Those with tots will be relieved

## HEY, KIDS!

Actor and comedian Robin Williams lives with his family in a mansion very near China Beach. You might see him out jogging if he isn't off somewhere making a film. Kids come from all over the city at Halloween to trick-or-treat at his house, hoping to catch a glimpse of Robin himself.

**KID-FRIENDLY EATS** There are no restaurants right next to China Beach, so the handiest thing to do is pack a picnic lunch or snacks or use the beach's barbecue facilities. For details on the Richmond District's **Bill's Place** (hamburgers) and **Ton Kiang** (Chinese food), *see* the California Palace of the Legion of Honor.

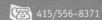

to know that strollers can be pushed all the way to the beach; look for the ramp on the left side. Nevertheless, despite being a prime beach for families, its location off the beaten track means that it seldom gets too crowded.

The facilities are good here, too. You'll find free changing rooms, showers, rest rooms, barbecue pits, picnic tables, and—if lying on sand isn't your thing—an enclosed sundeck for stretching out on your beach towel. Though small compared to other beaches, China Beach still has room to toss a Frisbee around, and you'll be treated to views of the Golden Gate and the Marin Headlands that match the million-dollar price tags of the homes perched above. You might even spot a marine mammal or two—perhaps a sea lion or a daredevil surfer (the human variety).

**TRANSPORTATION** To reach the somewhat-elusive China Beach, take El Camino del Mar to the area around Seacliff Avenue and 26th Avenue. Park in the small lot (which fills up early on weekends) or on the street, and walk down the hill. The No. 1 California bus stops a few blocks away. If you pull out a map and see the name James D. Phelan Beach in this location, don't worry that you're lost; that's just an older name for China Beach.

# CHINATOWN

Chinatown can be magical for kids: Neon signs, pagoda roofs, dragon-entwined lampposts, and shops packed with strange-looking herbs all add to its exotic allure. One of the largest Chinese communities outside Asia, it's a tightly packed, colorful 24-block jumble of restaurants, teahouses, temples, souvenir shops, and markets.

The only way to see the area is on foot. Start at the green-tiled, dragon-topped Chinatown Gate (Bush St. and Grant Ave.). It's much like entering a city within a city. Walk north up Grant Avenue—Chinatown's main thoroughfare—lined with bazaars, restaurants, and curio shops. But don't limit yourself to Grant. To the west, Stockton Street (where Chinese shop for produce and fresh fish) has a more authentic feel, as do many small alleyways nearby.

The Chinese Six Companies Building (843 Stockton St.), with curved roof tiles and pagoda top, should catch your kids' eye. Along narrow side streets like Hang Ah, Spofford Lane, and Ross Alley, you can hear the click of mah-jongg tiles, the whir of sewing machines, and the

**HEY, KIDS!** Chinatown is a great place to shop for friends, or for yourself. Many stores (especially along Grant Avenue) display baskets filled with toys and other inexpensive Chinese imports, right out on the sidewalk. Look for things like embroidered coin purses, silk fans, and little address books. Can we interest you in some dried lizards or other exotic herb or medicinal?

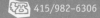 Bounded by Columbus Ave. and Bush, Kearny, Vallejo, and Powell Sts.

 Free

 Daily 24 hrs

415/982–6306

 5 and up

clinking of teacups. At the Golden Gate Fortune Cookie Factory (56 Ross Alley, tel. 415/781–3956), your kids can discover how fortunes get inside.

The Tien Hou Temple (125 Waverly Pl.) is the oldest Buddhist temple in the United States; climb to the third floor, where the air is redolent of incense and the decor features red-and-gold lanterns and carved wooden deities. The Chinese Culture Center, in the Holiday Inn (750 Kearny Street, tel. 415/986–1822), presents small exhibitions; it's fun to walk over Kearny via the footbridge. The best museum is the Chinese Historical Society of America (644 Broadway, Suite 402, tel. 415/391–1188), which documents the history of Chinese immigrants and their descendants. It's moving to 965 Clay Street in late 2000. At Portsmouth Square, site of an early settlement, elders greet the morning with tai chi exercises. Men then play cards and a Chinese version of chess, while grandmothers watch children on the playground. It's life, Chinese-American style.

**KID-FRIENDLY EATS** For a snack, get almond cookies, moon cakes, or steamed pork buns at a Chinese bakery, or buy fortune cookies. For lunch, try dim sum (filled dumplings and other small dishes, usually chosen from carts wheeled from table to table). **New Asia** (772 Pacific Ave., tel. 415/391–6666) and **Pearl City** (641 Jackson St., tel. 415/398–8383) are both good choices.

**KEEP IN MIND** The Chinese New Year Parade (tel. 415/391–9680), held each February or early March, is one of few remaining illuminated night parades. Some 500,000 spectators pack Chinatown and the Financial District to watch marching bands, floats, lion dancers, martial artists, acrobats, towering Chinese deities, and Gum Lum, a 200-foot-long Golden Dragon with 35 dancers inside. Firecrackers may frighten young children, however. The Chinatown Street Fair, the same weekend, features kite-making, lion dancing, and calligraphy.

# CLIFF HOUSE

Historic Cliff House, perched above the Pacific at San Francisco's westernmost tip, has knockout views of land and sea, making it a standard tour bus stop. From here, if they can see past the crowds, your children can watch (and listen to) sea lions basking and barking on the offshore Seal Rocks. These beasts come here October–June (contrary to rumor, not all have migrated to Pier 39), but ironically, seals—similar in appearance but otherwise different from sea lions—hardly ever come to the rocks named for them. To the south, Ocean Beach stretches 4 miles to Ft. Funston (*see* separate listings for these other sights).

Just north, you can gaze down at the ruins of the Sutro Baths, which, from 1896 until they burned down 70 years later, formed the world's largest indoor swimming pool—seven saltwater pools and three levels of galleries covered by a glass roof. Today you can walk along the foundations, which resemble Roman ruins, and imagine 20,000 people swimming here at once. Watch young kids carefully if you venture among the ruins.

## HEY, KIDS!

It's hard to resist the Musée Mécanique's games, but don't miss some of its other attractions: the miniature amusement park made of toothpicks by San Quentin inmates, or Laughing Sal, a mechanical lady who once cackled at a seaside amusement park nearby.

## KEEP IN MIND
Just across the Great Highway (atop the cliffs) from the Cliff House lies magnificent but often overlooked Sutro Heights Park, where old-time millionaire Adolph Sutro's mansion once stood. (Sutro, who made his fortune in the Gold Rush, was the same man who built the Sutro Baths.) The park has more great ocean views, picnic tables, shade trees, paths, and gardens. Enter either from Point Lobos Avenue or at Balboa Street across from the end of La Playa.

1090 Point Lobos Ave., at Great Hwy.

415/556–8642 visitor center,
415/386–1170 Musée Mécanique

Free, camera
obscura $1

Visitor center daily 10–5; museum M–F 11–7
(10–8 Memorial Day–Labor Day), Sa–Su 10–8

2 and up

The Cliff House itself, built in 1909, is the third on this site since 1863. Today it houses a popular restaurant and bar and an adjacent visitor center, whose historical and natural history displays include fascinating old photos of both previous Cliff House incarnations, which burned down. The first hosted dignitaries and wealthy residents, who drove their carriages out to the beach; the second and most luxurious rose eight stories and had a 200-foot-high observation tower.

Near the visitor center is the Musée Mécanique, a quirky penny arcade—quarters are today's currency—with mechanical games old and new. It brims with player pianos, pinball machines, and nickelodeons. Just outside is an unusual camera obscura, a replica of an invention by Leonardo Da Vinci. Its lens displays images from outside on a matte-finish dish inside. You might see people on the beach below, or, on a clear day, the Farallon Islands, 27 miles offshore. At press time, however, the camera's future was threatened by plans to expand the Cliff House.

**KID-FRIENDLY EATS** You can picnic at Sutro Heights Park or Ocean Beach. **Cliff House** (tel. 415/386–3330) is geared to tourists, but you can't knock the views. Dining is either upstairs (best for breakfasts and light lunches) or in the downstairs dining room, specializing in seafood. Kids can order small portions. There's also a deli and hot dog stand. **Louis'** (902 Point Lobos Ave., tel. 415/387–6330), overlooking the Pacific and the Sutro Baths, serves diner food to happy locals, and you won't pay extra for the views.

# COIT TOWER AND TELEGRAPH HILL

Folklore has it that 210-foot Coit Tower, which crowns the crest of 248-foot Telegraph Hill, was built to resemble the end of a fire hose. While this may be a myth, there's some logic to it: The stone-white concrete tower was intended as a monument to the city's volunteer firefighters. (Lillie Hitchcock Coit, who bequeathed the funds that paid for it, was a wealthy and eccentric heiress with a passion for fire engines—and firemen.) Since 1933, when it was completed, the tower has become one of San Francisco's most distinctive landmarks—with only the Golden Gate Bridge and perhaps the Transamerica Pyramid more recognized as symbols of the city.

Coit Tower also offers some of San Francisco's best views—an exciting panorama of hills, islands, bridges, and the bay spreading out below. The 360° vista from the top of the tower's Observation Gallery, reached by elevator, is the most encompassing; however, if you come in the evening after the Observation Gallery has closed—when the tower is lit up like a beacon—or you don't want to ride to the top, you can simply drink in the free views outside. Inside

**KID-FRIENDLY EATS** **Tommaso's** (1042 Kearny St., tel. 415/398–9696) crisp, thin-crust pizzas may be San Francisco's all-time favorite. You may have to wait for a table, so come early (dinner only; no reservations). If you walk down from Telegraph Hill via the Filbert or Greenwich steps, you'll land close to the well-known, upscale **Fog City Diner** (1300 Battery St., at the Embarcadero, tel. 415/982–2000). Families can share a variety of "small plates" or opt for burgers and shakes.

Telegraph Hill Blvd., at Greenwich or Lombard Sts.

415/362-0808

Observation Gallery
$3.75 ages 13 and up,
$1.50 children 6–12

Observation Gallery daily 10–7:30

6 and up

the tower, on the ground floor, are murals that were painted by 25 artists as a public works project during the Depression; these depict California's working people in a socialist-realist style pioneered by Mexican artist Diego Rivera.

If you've walked or taken the bus to the top of Telegraph Hill, you can opt for either of two easy-to-overlook routes down that provide intriguing glimpses into a hidden corner of the city, as well as more great views of the bay. The Filbert Steps and Greenwich Steps, both steep staircase walks that parallel each other as they lead down toward the bay from the east side of Telegraph Hill, are flanked by terraced gardens and secluded homes.

**HEY, KIDS!** How did Telegraph Hill get its name? It was once known as Signal Hill for the semaphore (a flag or other type of visual signaling device) placed atop it in 1850, which let local merchants know that ships were arriving. But when the West Coast's first telegraph station was built here in 1853, it became Telegraph Hill.

**TRANSPORTATION** The easiest way to walk to the tower is via Lombard Street (not the famous crooked part) and up a flight of steps, but the steep climb can be taxing. An alternative is the No. 39 Coit bus, which leaves from Washington Square. If you drive up, you may be in for a headache. Parking is tight and the lot at the top is often filled, which can result in a long, frustrating traffic tie-up with no way to turn back.

# COYOTE POINT PARK AND MUSEUM

On a sunny weekend day, it's a good idea to arrive early to beat the crowds at Coyote Point Park, a bay-side recreational area of greenery and sand about 2 miles south of San Francisco International Airport, across U.S. 101 from the town of Burlingame. Coyote Point has a lot going for it. You'll find tree-shaded walking trails with bay overlooks, bike paths, picnic areas, playfields and playgrounds, a fishing jetty, a marina, a summer swimming beach, a saltwater marsh, an adjacent public golf course, and a modern, highly regarded nature museum. About the only thing lacking, besides roller coasters and pizza stands, is enough parking to accommodate all the family cars pouring in for a day's fun in the sunshine.

The Coyote Point Museum for Environmental Education, however, makes Coyote Point an all-weather destination. Even on a nice day, be sure to leave some time for it. Here, your kids can see live animals native to the Bay Area displayed in realistic habitats. Look for river otters, burrowing owls, porcupines, badgers, skunks, birds of prey, toads, snakes,

## HEY, KIDS!
Coyote Point Museum offers five-day Summer Discovery Camps for kids aged 7–10. Over the course of the week, you get to meet animals, go tide-pooling at an ocean beach, and go hiking, too. If you're interested, ask your parents to call the park for more information.

**KEEP IN MIND** Pick up a flyer of current museum events for families, which might include Family Fun Festivals (parties overlooking the bay) and occasional Wild Wednesdays, when the museum stays open late to better showcase nocturnal animals. Also check to see what temporary exhibitions the museum is showing; they often include wild animals and hands-on displays for kids and may warrant a return visit all by themselves.

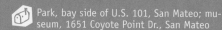
Park, bay side of U.S. 101, San Mateo; museum, 1651 Coyote Point Dr., San Mateo

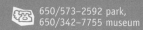
650/573-2592 park,
650/342-7755 museum

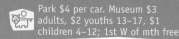
Park $4 per car. Museum $3 adults, $2 youths 13-17, $1 children 4-12; 1st W of mth free

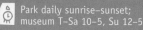
Park daily sunrise-sunset; museum T-Sa 10-5, Su 12-5

All ages

lizards, bobcats—even lowly banana slugs. A walk-through outdoor aviary provides close-up looks at a variety of birds.

In addition to lots of light and space and fun-to-follow wooden ramps connecting the displays, the museum contains computer games, interactive exhibits, and an Environmental Hall that leads you through the Bay Area's major ecosystems: redwood forest, chaparral, grasslands, oak woodlands, and coastal. It's like taking a walk from the Santa Cruz Mountains to the Pacific Ocean (but a lot easier on your feet). While the museum is especially well suited to school-age kids, any child 3 or over can enjoy the displays. A well-stocked nature store is attached.

**KID-FRIENDLY EATS** The park contains several picnic areas. For restaurants in nearby Burlingame, *see* the Burlingame Museum of Pez Memorabilia. Come to think of it, why not combine a trip here with a trip there and snack on some Pez candies along the way?

# THE EMBARCADERO

I f San Francisco's destructive 1989 earthquake had one positive effect, it was—by near-unanimous agreement today—the subsequent tearing down of the quake-damaged Embarcadero Freeway. For decades, that elevated river of concrete had obscured bay views and blocked the sunlight along this 3-mi bay-side route. With the freeway gone, the area has blossomed into a promenade for walkers, joggers, rollerbladers, renegade skateboarders, sun worshipers, restaurant-goers, and those who simply wish to gaze out at the endless procession of sailboats, tugboats, barges, freighters, ferries, cruise ships—and the occasional submarine—on their way from port to port or out to sea.

The centerpiece of the Embarcadero, at the foot of Market Street, is the historic Ferry Building, built at the turn of the 20th century. Its 230-foot clock tower was once the tallest structure west of the Mississippi and, illuminated at night, remains a recognizable city landmark. Until 1958, 170 ferries disembarked here daily, and it remains a departure point for ferries

**HEY, KIDS!** Before bridges spanned the bay connecting San Francisco to the East Bay and Marin County, some 100,000 ferryboat commuters used to pass through the Ferry Building every day. It was the main gateway to the city and the second-busiest passenger terminal in the world. Close your eyes and imagine all the hustle and bustle. Then open your eyes and see today's activity.

The Embarcadero, from China
Basin to Fisherman's Wharf

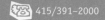 415/391–2000

Free

Daily 24 hrs

 5 and up

to Oakland, Sausalito, Larkspur, and Vallejo (*see* Bay Cruises). Walk to the plaza behind the Ferry Building for good views of the bay, the ferries, and the Bay Bridge.

The Embarcadero is lined with piers, some still in use for shipping, most now put to other purposes (or none at all). South of the Ferry Building, all piers are even numbered; to the north, piers are odd numbered. The best known is Pier 39 (*see below*), now a seaside shopping mall. The lesser-known Pier 7, just north of the Ferry Building, was once a passenger pier but has been converted into a public promenade lined with vintage lampposts and benches. Its wooden-plank pier, the city's longest, is ideal for eating a picnic lunch and gazing out to sea. Your children may enjoy watching anglers at the end, pulling up flounder, kingfish, even leopard shark. Another good spot is South Beach Harbor, just south of Pier 40, where you can check out the yachts and the views from south of the Bay Bridge.

**TRANSPORTATION** Muni streetcars (an extension of the N. Judah Line) travel down the Embarcadero from Market Street to China Basin. With area parking tight, it's a handy alternative to driving. Fares are $1 adults, 35¢ kids 5–17, and you get a free transfer, good for 90 minutes. To get here by cable car, ride the California Street line to the foot of Market.

**KID-FRIENDLY EATS** Many attractions in the vicinity of the Embarcadero are covered under their own listings. So for suggested nearby restaurants (not to mention other activities to combine with a visit here), check out the profiles of Alcatraz Island, Coit Tower and Telegraph Hill, Embarcadero Center, Fisherman's Wharf, the International Children's Art Museum, Liberty Ship *Jeremiah O'Brien,* and Pier 39.

# EMBARCADERO CENTER

**41**

The five skyscrapers that make up Embarcadero Center, sometimes dubbed "Rockefeller Center West," range over 10 acres and eight city blocks. They house more than 100 shops, 40 restaurants, a five-screen movie theater, two hotels, and a 41st-floor indoor-outdoor observation area. Though offices fill the upper stories of four of the towers, their three lower tiers are lined with shops and restaurants and connected by a series of walkways and bridges leading to plazas, fountains, and landscaped gardens.

Embarcadero Center's biggest tourist draw may be SkyDeck, San Francisco's only indoor-outdoor observatory, located atop One Embarcadero Center (the farthest tower from the bay). The view from the semi-open-air observation deck is like looking through a big picture window at the bay and city skyline, 565 feet above ground. You can see the Bay Bridge, Treasure Island, the Transamerica Pyramid, Coit Tower, Alcatraz, Angel Island, and Oakland. Inside, watch videos about San Francisco history. Before plopping down your cash, however, remember that there are plenty of free vantage points around the city—though few quite so high.

## HEY, KIDS!

Every minute, 30,000 gallons of water fall from the Justin Herman Plaza's 30-foot-wide Vallaincourt Fountain into a reflecting pool. Walkways are built into the fountain sculpture, so you can walk under and around the waterfalls—great on a hot day (a rarity in foggy San Francisco).

## KID-FRIENDLY EATS

Sacramento Alley, alongside Four Embarcadero Center just off Justin Herman Plaza, has several good takeout eateries. (Eat at a nearby table or bench, and you might chance upon a free concert.) **Chili Up!** (tel. 415/576–0811) serves several types of chili, including black-bean chicken, Texas-style without beans, and ancho (a chili) turkey with pinto beans. **Metro** (tel. 415/986–2406) dishes up a variety of sausage sandwiches and hot dogs, as well as other sandwiches. Other takeout places specialize in sushi, pizza, and soups and salads.

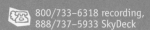

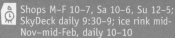
A more unlikely, but definitely cheaper, sightseeing attraction is the Hyatt Regency Hotel, the center's "fifth" skyscraper (and the one closest to the bay). Even if you have no intention of staying there, stop in for a peek. The hotel's pyramid-shape, 17-story-high atrium lobby is ringed by balconies, topped by a skylight, and enlivened by full-size trees, hanging gardens, and fountains. Be sure to take your kids for a ride on one of the glass elevators that whisk you up the inside of the "pyramid."

In winter, an outdoor ice rink in adjacent Justin Herman Plaza provides plenty of action.

**TRANSPORTATION** You can ride the California Street cable car line to Embarcadero Center (get off at the last stop, near the foot of Market Street). If you drive, you can park in one of the underground garages and get free validated parking on weekends after 10 AM or on weekdays after 5 PM from selected restaurants or the Embarcadero Center Cinema.

# EXPLORATORIUM

Most kids' eyes light up as soon as they enter the Exploratorium, which bills itself as a "mad scientist's penny arcade, scientific fun house, and experimental laboratory all rolled into one." Set within the cavernous inner sanctum of the Palace of Fine Arts, in the Marina District, it's one of the world's top science museums, drawing 600,000 visitors per year. More than 650 hands-on exhibits invite curious kids and parents to test and investigate mysteries of science and human perception—how we see, hear, smell, and feel the world around us. Light, color, sound, music, motion, language, electricity, and weather are among the subject areas.

What's that cloud ring rising into the air? A 5-year-old boy made it in the Weather area. How did that 7-year-old girl leave her shadow on the wall? Your kids can capture their own shadows in the Shadow Box. Look at that 10-year-old—he's as tall as the ceiling! (But only in the Distorted Room.) How did that family make the Enchanted Tree light up? Just by clapping their hands. "Explainers"—often high-school students on their days off—offer help and

**KEEP IN MIND** The Exploratorium is housed within the Palace of Fine Arts. This neoclassical domed and pillared beauty built for the 1915 Panama-Pacific International Exhibition—and the only structure still surviving from it—rises alongside a lovely tree-shaded lagoon occupied by mallards and swans. Benches and sloping grassy hillsides provide space for resting and sunning before or after visiting the Exploratorium, and your kids can feed the ducks. The Exploratorium is one of the attractions covered by CityPass (*see* the California Academy of Sciences).

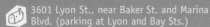

3601 Lyon St., near Baker St. and Marina Blvd. (parking at Lyon and Bay Sts.)

415/561-0360, 415/561-0362 Tactile Dome reservations

$9 adults, $7 college students, $5 youths 6–17, $2.50 children 3–5; 1st W of mth free

Memorial Day–Labor Day, Th–T 10–6, W 10–9; otherwise T and Th–Su 10–5, W 10–9:30

2 and up

demonstrations ("Cow-eye dissection starting over here!"). Besides the Exploratorium's permanent exhibits, two or three intriguing temporary exhibits go on display each year—on such varied topics as the process of memory or the intricacies of flea circuses.

A separate area, the Tactile Dome, requires reservations (one to six weeks in advance), an additional fee, and a sense of adventure. In this pitch-black maze set inside a geodesic dome, the challenge—and the fun—is to crawl, slide, and climb through it relying entirely on your sense of touch. (It's not recommended for kids under 7, pregnant women, or the claustrophobic.) It takes about 15 minutes to work your way through once, but many go through two or three times (you're allotted 1 hour and 15 minutes). By then your child will be ready to come back into the light and experience all five senses at this extraordinary museum.

**HEY, KIDS!** While you're here, be sure to try finger painting via computer. You can use more than 1,000 different computer-generated digital colors. Don't forget to reach out and touch a miniature tornado and blow giant soap bubbles, too. And if you brought some money, you may want to check out the museum store, which is filled with science-minded toys, books, and gadgets.

**KID-FRIENDLY EATS** The **Exploratorium Café** (tel. 415/921–8603) serves such items as organic salads and tuna or smoked turkey sandwiches for lunch. At noisy and colorful **Café Marimba** (2317 Chestnut St., tel. 415/776–1506), the Oaxacan-style Mexican food includes family-size platters of grilled chicken or pork ribs, seafood tacos, and kid-pleasing quesadillas. **Mels Drive-In** (2165 Lombard St., tel. 415/921–2867) serves up burgers, curly fries, milk shakes, and cherry Cokes with '50s decor and jukeboxes. Kids' meals come in toy Corvettes.

# FARALLON NATIONAL
## WILDLIFE REFUGE

On a clear day, from points along the western edges of San Francisco, you can usually see the Farallon Islands jutting up from the Pacific, 27 miles off the Golden Gate. Even most longtime San Franciscans, however, have never seen the Farallones close up—or have a clue as to the extraordinary display of wildlife that's out there. The seven islands' rocky slopes are home to 23 species of marine mammals, including thousands of harbor seals, California sea lions, Steller's sea lions, and Northern elephant seals. And up to 300,000 breeding seabirds visit the islands annually—making this the largest Pacific seabird rookery south of Alaska.

A maximum of eight people, all researchers, are allowed on the refuge at a time. The public isn't allowed to set foot in this fragile environment—sometimes called "the most exclusive neighborhood in San Francisco" (the islands are within city and county limits). But you can get excellent views from the deck of an Oceanic Society Expeditions boat.

The eight-hour Farallon Island Nature Cruise (reservations required), aboard a 63-foot

## HEY, KIDS!
Keep a sharp eye out for whales spouting (the spouts look like puffs of smoke), which may mean they're going to surface. If you spot one, let the naturalist on board know about it, so he or she can alert the other passengers. And feel free to ask questions or point out other things you see.

**KEEP IN MIND** This is a trip you definitely need to prepare for ahead of time. Make sure everyone in your party dresses warmly and waterproofed—trips depart rain or shine. Be certain of your children's seaworthiness before embarking, as there's no turning back. Kids should have sailed on the ocean at least once before going. Take seasickness precautions, and bring binoculars, sunglasses, and sunscreen. You're likely to encounter less foggy weather in fall than in summer.

 Oceanic Society Expeditions, Ft. Mason Center, Bldg. E

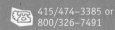 415/474–3385 or 800/326-7491

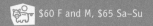 $60 F and M, $65 Sa–Su

 Boats depart 8 AM F–Su, June–Nov; arrive half hour early

 10 and up

Coast Guard–certified vessel, departs from San Francisco's Ft. Mason (*see* Marina Green). The trip is for adults and children 10 and over only, since the seas can get rough and the winds very cold. Expert naturalists point out wildlife and answer questions. As you set out past the Golden Gate, you and your children may spot such birds as gulls, murres, pelicans, pigeon guillemots, double-crested cormorants, oystercatchers, rhinoceros auklets, albatrosses, and tufted puffins. Chances are a number of Dall porpoises will escort the boat, darting around, past, and under the bow in a sort of exhilarating joyride. Whales are a common sight: humpbacks with flukes shooting high in the air as they dive, and even blue whales, the largest mammals ever on earth. Pacific white-sided or Risso's dolphins are sometimes spotted, too. The granite islands themselves are alive with birds, their shrieking and squawking surrounding you in natural stereo, while a parcel of barking sea lions typically provides the basso profundo.

**KID-FRIENDLY EATS** You'll need to bring snacks, lunch, and drinks for the boat trip since there's no galley on board. For dinner, **Greens** (Ft. Mason Center, Bldg. A, tel. 415/771–6222) is an excellent vegetarian restaurant, good for older kids; it has terrific bay views, but you'll need reservations. **Café Marimba** (*see* the Exploratorium) serves creative Mexican cuisine.

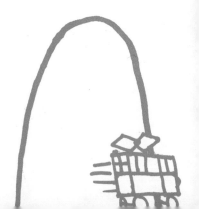

# FISHERMAN'S WHARF

Fisherman's Wharf is no longer the thriving fishing center it was a century ago. Modern-day catches have been ravaged by over-fishing and pollution. Today, the historic waterfront district, a now loosely defined area that runs for eight or nine blocks from Aquatic Park to Pier 39 (*see below*), relies mainly on tourism for revenues. Crowds can be overwhelming (come in the morning if possible), and the last remnants of the real working wharf can be hard to find amid the hodgepodge of attractions, some maritime-related, some not. These include schlocky souvenir stands and often-mediocre seafood restaurants. For all these reasons, many locals tend to avoid it. Still, the bay sparkles, boats are near at hand, you can get here by cable car, and it's a colorful, noisy, active place that kids tend to like.

To glimpse real fishermen at work, head for Richard Henry Dana Street (better known as "Fish Alley")—but remember that fishermen work early. Some other authentic sights at the Wharf are provided on a bevy of historic ships berthed there. The San Francisco Maritime National Historic Park (*see below*) includes a fascinating collection of boats at the Hyde Street Pier.

**KEEP IN MIND** Many kids seem irresistibly drawn to Wharf attractions that have nothing to do with local color. One of the better ones is a branch of Ripley's Believe It or Not! Museum (175 Jefferson St., tel. 415/771–6188), which chronicles the bizarre and un-usual with oddities such as a shrunken human torso, an 8-foot-long cable car built from match-sticks, and a portrait of Rudolph Valentino made from dryer lint.

The U.S.S. *Pampanito* (Pier 45, tel. 415/775– 1943) is a restored World War II submarine. Launched in 1943, the sub saw action in the Pacific and sank 27,000 tons of enemy shipping. Self-guided audio tours lead through the cramped crews' and officers' quarters, the engine rooms, and the torpedo room.

More commercial attractions, which have little to do with the sea, line Jefferson Street. These places may be tourist traps, but that doesn't mean they can't be fun, especially for kids. Often, though, you can get plenty of entertainment at the Wharf without paying. A delightful collection of street performers— jugglers, musicians, magicians—usually may be found either on the streets or at the area's four main shopping centers: the Cannery and Ghirardelli Square, Pier 39 (*see* listings for both), and the Anchorage.

**HEY, KIDS!** The Wharf is the site of a Big July 4 Waterfront Festival (tel. 415/777–7120), which ends with fireworks around 9:30. There's a children's stage and other stages for live music and entertainment, plus plenty of food booths. Tell Mom and Dad to be sure to pack sweatshirts for the fog.

**KID-FRIENDLY EATS** It's hard to resist the stands with bubbling crab pots on Jefferson Street for a crab or shrimp cocktail, even if many are skimpy and overpriced. Two good fish restaurants are **A. Sabella's** (2766 Taylor St., tel. 415/771–4416), which serves seafood and pasta with an extensive children's menu, and **Alioto's** (8 Fisherman's Wharf, tel. 415/673–0183), which has old-time atmosphere and seafood that really does match the views. For burgers, fries, and shakes, try **Johnny Rockets** (81 Jefferson St., tel. 415/693– 9120).

# FT. FUNSTON

**43**

Where's the fort at Ft. Funston? If you're looking for a walled fortress, cannons, and all the other things you normally associate with forts, try Fort Point National Historic Site (*see below*) in the Presidio. The military did, however, once stake a claim to this area of windswept sands just south of Ocean Beach (*see below*), along the western reaches of San Francisco. The last of the undeveloped dunes that once blanketed much of the coast are still preserved here.

Since the early 1900s, and through two world wars, the Army used the high cliffs at Ft. Funston as a strategic lookout and a base for heavy weaponry protecting San Francisco Bay from attack. During World War II, Ft. Funston's Battery Davis sported guns weighing almost 150 tons each. During the Cold War, the current parking lot was the site of a Nike missile battery. But since the Army pulled out some years ago, all that remains of its legacy are gun emplacements gathering rust in the foggy mists.

**KID-FRIENDLY EATS** There are picnic tables but no food concessions here. Among the closest restaurants are the **Boathouse** (*see* Lake Merced) and **Leon's Bar-B-Q** (2800 Sloat Blvd., tel. 415/681–3071), near the zoo, dishing up ribs, jambalaya, and sweet potato pie.

**KEEP IN MIND** While rare, crashes have occurred at the hang-gliding observation deck, so it's a good idea to keep an eye out—and up. Some other safety suggestions: In general, keep your kids away from cliff edges, and beware of rip tides at the beach. As for comfort, it can get very foggy here, so dress yourself and your children in layers. Nothing ruins an outing faster than cold kids.

Skyline Blvd. off Great Hwy. or John Muir Dr.

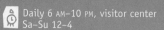 415/556–8371, 415/333–0100
weather hot line for hang gliders

 Free

 Daily 6 AM–10 PM, visitor center
Sa–Su 12–4

5 and up

Today, Ft. Funston is part of the Golden Gate National Recreation Area, and where guns once pointed out to the Pacific, rangers and volunteers now run a nursery for native plants and lead environmental education programs for schoolkids. You and your children can hike to the beach below or watch from a viewing deck as hang gliders take off from the cliffs and soar through the skies. (This is the most popular hang-gliding spot in the city.) The Sunset Trail, a 1-mile paved loop, traverses the cliffs and provides sea views; as its name suggests, this is one of the best places in San Francisco to watch the sun go down. The trail links up to the Coastal Trail going north along Ocean Beach, and on clear days you can see up to Marin County. Stay on marked trails: Some of the roads you may see here actually go nowhere. They were built to confuse the enemy in wartime, but thankfully, no enemies ever invaded.

HEY, KIDS! Much of the vegetation—ice plant, acacia, eucalyptus, and Monterey cypress trees—that you see along the trail was planted here by the Army to provide camouflage, or disguise, for the gun batteries at Ft. Funston as well as to control soil erosion. Rangers are now trying to get rid of some of it to make room for native plants, like sticky monkey flower and beach sagewort. Check out the greenhouse near the visitor center to see what these plants look like.

# FORT POINT NATIONAL
## HISTORIC SITE

Dramatically situated beneath the southern stretches of the Golden Gate Bridge on San Francisco Bay, Ft. Point is the only brick fort you can visit in the western United States. Built during the Civil War to help protect San Francisco from sea attack—it was modeled after Ft. Sumter in South Carolina and completed in 1861—the massive fort could hold as many as 500 soldiers and 126 cannons. During World War II, soldiers stood watch here as part of the coastal defense of California. Today it's part of Presidio National Park (*see below*) and a good place to immerse kids in some local military history while soaking up breathtaking vistas of the bay below and the bridge overhead.

The best views are from the roof of the fort, where your kids can pretend they're searching for enemy ships. More likely, they'll spot windsurfers braving the waves here or freighters passing through the Golden Gate. Just to the east, where the surf crashes into the rocks below the walkway, is the spot where Jimmy Stewart pulled Kim Novak out of the water in the Hitchcock film *Vertigo* (a good video to watch with older kids before visiting).

**HEY, KIDS!** When the rangers ask for volunteers to help load the cannons, you might want to join in. If you do, you'll receive a special cannoneer certificate. You don't need to worry about getting hit by a cannonball—or even loud noises—since the cannons aren't actually fired, and no live ammo is used. Volunteers each do one job: cleaning the cannon, loading the charge, relaying the ammo, firing (actually, pretending to fire), etc. All ages are welcome.

 Marine Dr., off Long Ave. and
Lincoln Blvd., the Presidio

 Free

 W–Su 10–5

 415/556–1693

6 and up

Even though Ft. Point was well equipped with cannons, none have ever been fired in anger here. But national park rangers conduct cannon-loading demonstrations on an 1862-era field artillery piece every day, and it's a complex, fascinating process. (Call the fort for the daily schedule.) Sometimes, on busy weekends and holidays, docents dressed in Civil War–era costumes give tours, adding to the historical flavor. Your family can also visit the rooms that lie off the restored central courtyard to see museum-style exhibits of American military memorabilia and watch a film containing old newsreel footage of the building of the Golden Gate Bridge. It all makes for an outing that's both informative and entertaining at a site both strategic and stunning.

## KEEP IN MIND
National Park Service rangers lead weekend walking tours of Ft. Point and other former military installations in the Presidio—best for kids 10 and up. The Presidio Visitors Information Center (*see* Presidio National Park), open daily 10–5, has schedules, along with maps, brochures, and trail guides of the area.

**KID-FRIENDLY EATS** The Presidio's branch of **Burger King** (211 Lincoln Blvd., tel. 415/673–1856) is like any other Burger King except that it has one of the best views of the Golden Gate Bridge of any restaurant in the city; it's also the closest eating place to Ft. Point. For restaurants in the nearby Richmond District (follow Lincoln Boulevard west to 25th Avenue), *see* the California Palace of the Legion of Honor; for Marina District eateries, just east of the Presidio, *see* the Exploratorium.

# GOLDEN GATE BRIDGE

**41**

It's the symbol of San Francisco and probably the most celebrated and photographed bridge in the world. Completed in 1937 after four years of construction, the Golden Gate Bridge is still one of the world's longest suspension bridges, stretching across the straits (aka the Golden Gate) from San Francisco north to Marin County. Its two towers rise 750 feet into the air and it uses enough cable wire to wrap around the equator three times. More than 40 million vehicles cross it each year. You can drive across the bridge, too, of course, but the best way to see it—and the views from it—is to walk or bike across.

If you're walking, park your car either at the lot on the San Francisco side or at Vista Point, on the Marin side, and set out. Though the bridge is 1.7 miles long (including approaches), you don't need to cover the full distance to get the full effect. It's a thrill just to get a few hundred feet out onto the bridge, which stands 220 feet above the water. You'll feel the rush of air as cars whiz by and feel the bridge sway in the wind. (In fact, it can sway as much as 27½ feet east to west.) Linger as long as you want—and as your kids will allow—

## KEEP IN MIND
Make sure everyone dresses warmly, even on sunny days, because the winds can whip fiercely across the bridge and you never know when the damp fog will come swirling in. If parking your car, bring plenty of quarters for the parking meters.

## HEY, KIDS!
When you're walking on the bridge, look up toward the cables to try to spot painters on the walkways. The bridge takes four years to paint—a process that never ends. As soon as they finish, they start all over again. Some kids—and adults, too—are surprised that the bridge isn't painted gold to match its name. Its reddish-orange color, called "International Orange," was chosen because it's easiest to see in the fog, helping planes and birds avoid collisions.

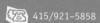

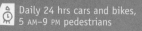

Rte. 1 and U.S. 101 north (from Marina, take Doyle Dr. from Richardson Ave. or Marina Blvd.)

415/921–5858

Pedestrians, bikes, and northbound cars free; southbound cars $3

Daily 24 hrs cars and bikes, 5 AM–9 PM pedestrians

All ages

to see the views of the city skyline, Alcatraz, Angel Island, Ft. Point, the Marin Headlands, and a passing parade of sailboats, freighters, and windsurfers. Times when fog is swirling about are especially magical.

If you are riding bikes, you'll be limited to the west (ocean) side of the bridge on weekends and weekday evenings; pedestrians use the east (bay side) walkway. Experienced cyclists might consider continuing to Sausalito in Marin County for more bay-side views or to explore the town. Just follow the bike lane at the end of the Vista Point parking lot to Alexander Avenue, but realize that once off the bridge, you'll be sharing the road with cars.

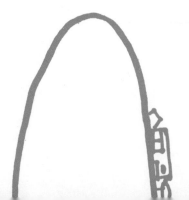

**KID-FRIENDLY EATS** The nearest restaurants are in the Richmond and Marina districts. **Ton Kiang** (*see* the California Palace of the Legion of Honor), in the Richmond District, serves some of the best Chinese food in the city. **Giorgio's Pizzeria** (151 Clement St., tel. 415/668–1266), also in the Richmond, is a longtime contender for best pizza in San Francisco. For information on **Mels Drive-In** and **Café Marimba,** in the Marina District, *see* the Exploratorium.

# GOLDEN GATE PARK

**40**

You could probably spend every weekend for a year in 3-mile-long, ½-mile-wide Golden Gate Park and still miss at least one corner of it. Though fraying a bit around the edges—cutbacks in public funds mean fewer gardeners and maintenance people and more homeless "campers"—this remains one of America's most beautiful urban parks, filled with lakes, flowers, and meadows.

Most attractions are clustered in the eastern half of the park, including some of the city's top museums: the M.H. de Young Memorial Museum and the California Academy of Sciences (*see* listings for both). Lying between them is the Music Concourse, where the park band plays free concerts on Sunday afternoons. Next to the de Young is the Japanese Tea Garden, with arched bridges, koi fish ponds, and a towering red pagoda. Across the road is Strybing Arboretum and Botanical Gardens, which displays flowers, redwoods, cacti, and other flora from around the world; don't miss the duck pond near the entrance.

**HEY, KIDS!** With a bike or Rollerblades (there are lots of rental places nearby), you can take advantage of the park's more than 7 miles of paved roads and trails. One of the best times to ride is Sundays, when Kennedy Drive is closed to cars between Stanyan Street and 19th Avenue and bicyclists and in-line skaters take over. At 6th Avenue and Fulton Street, a flat paved area draws flashy skaters who jump and do dance steps to lively music.

Bounded by Fulton and Stanyan Sts.,
Lincoln Way, and Great Hwy.

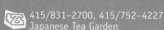
415/831–2700, 415/752–4227
Japanese Tea Garden

Free; some
attractions charge

Daily 6 AM–10 PM

All ages

Just up Martin Luther King Jr. Drive is pretty Stow Lake, where you can picnic and rent rowboats, paddleboats, or electric boats. Cross footbridges to hilly Strawberry Island, in the middle of the lake, and hike to the top to peer over the crest of Huntington Falls, which plunges 125 feet—the West's highest artificial waterfall. Nearby, the Rhododendron Dell blazes with color in spring. In the park's southeast corner, the Children's Playground (off Kezar or Bowling Green Drs.) contains swings, slides, and climbing structures, and the adjacent 1912 Herschel-Spillman Carousel spins with 62 hand-carved animals. The park's western half is more woodsy and pastoral; toward the ocean (along Kennedy Drive), you can visit a herd of bison at the Bison Paddock and hike, bike, or stroll along quiet tree-lined trails.

The park also contains horse trails and stables, a par-3 golf course, tennis courts, horseshoe pits, lawn-bowling greens, handball courts, ball fields, fly-casting pools, dog runs, a polo field, and an archery field.

**KID-FRIENDLY EATS** Staff in traditional costume serve tea at the **Teahouse** (Japanese Tea Garden, Tea Garden Dr., tel. 415/752–1171), where the fortune cookie reputedly was invented. The **Beach Chalet** (1000 Great Hwy., tel. 415/386–8439), an often crowded brew pub, serves up buffalo wings, gumbo, and great views. Also see California Academy of Sciences.

**KEEP IN MIND** Pick up a park map at McLaren Lodge (Stanyan and Fell Sts.), open weekdays 8–5, or at the Beach Chalet visitor center at the far western end of the park. You can buy a Golden Gate Park Explorer Pass (see the California Academy of Sciences), good for one-time adult admission to park museums and the Japanese Tea Garden, plus other discounts, but there's no Explorer Pass for kids.

# INTERNATIONAL CHILDREN'S
## ART MUSEUM

**W**hen this three-room museum on the ground floor of the Ferry Building started up in 1995, it became the first museum in the country devoted to international children's art.

It serves as a display space and clearinghouse for an international art and writing exchange program called "Paint Brush Diplomacy," in which students from American classrooms are matched with students from around the world. The program's mission is to have kids communicate with their peers and gain deeper global understanding through art. While the pictures reveal differences in cultures, landscapes, housing, and other aspects of life, they also show what kids around the globe have in common—family, school, religion, pets, and love of nature, to name a few.

Some of the pictures received from classrooms abroad are added to the museum's ever-growing permanent collection, which consists of more than 4,000 artworks from more than 100 countries.

**KEEP IN MIND** The Ferry Building remains a departure point for ferries to Oakland, Sausalito, Larkspur, and Vallejo. Walk to the plaza behind the building for good views of the bay, the ferries, and the Bay Bridge, or take a boat ride after visiting the museum. To find out about ferry trips, *see* Bay Cruises.

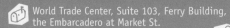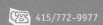 World Trade Center, Suite 103, Ferry Building, the Embarcadero at Market St.

415/772-9977

 $1 adults, 50¢ children 18 and under; 1st Sa of mth free; art workshops free

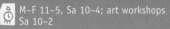 M–F 11–5, Sa 10–4; art workshops Sa 10–2

3 and up

Those chosen to go on display are nicely framed and shown in exhibits that rotate every three to four months in the main gallery. Look for kids' art from countries as diverse as Turkey, Kenya, Poland, Japan, Egypt, Lithuania, Chile, Cameroon, and India. You can suggest that your children search for glimpses of life that are both different from and similar to life in your own community. Pictures that aren't on display are available for viewing on CD-ROM. The museum also sets up traveling exhibits that visit other museums and cultural centers across the country.

But your kids can do more than just look at art here. They can create it, too. They'll find all the art supplies they need in the room called the Studio. (Kids can also put on their own puppet shows here.) On Saturday, the Studio also has drop-in Paint the World art workshops. Here children can create hands-on multicultural art projects, which they can take home; some artworks may even be selected for display in the Studio. Imagine how your kids would feel to have their work hung in a real museum!

KID-FRIENDLY EATS **Omar's Café** (World Trade Center #138, the Embarcadero, tel. 415/392–6627), in the Ferry Building, has deli sandwiches, bagels, soups, and Middle Eastern fare (falafel, Greek salad, and meze plates) served in informal surroundings. For other casual eateries in the area, see Embarcadero Center.

Japantown is the focal point for San Francisco's 12,000 citizens of Japanese descent, who first settled this area after the 1906 earthquake. As the Japanese built churches, shrines, shops, and restaurants, the neighborhood began to take on the look of a miniature Ginza and became known as Nihonmachi or Japantown. Its commercial heart is the Japan Center—a three-square-block complex of shops, restaurants, teahouses, hotels, pastry shops, movie theaters, a bowling alley, Japanese baths, and more, all connected by walkways. With the exception of a five-tiered, 100-foot-high pagoda crowning its Peace Plaza, a few fountains, and other touches, the Japan Center's design lacks traditional Japanese grace. But it's a fun place for kids to wander around, perhaps eyeing the plastic food displays in restaurant windows, shopping for cassettes, or leafing through Japanese books. They can also look for flying-fish kites, miniature notepads, and other colorful items from Japan in the shops.

A 135-foot covered bridge lined with shops and a restaurant crosses over Webster Street between two of the commercial buildings. It's a wonderful spot to browse, as is the Buchanan Mall,

**HEY, KIDS!** The Japantown Bowl (1790 Post St., tel. 415/921–6200, 415/575–2902 reservations), in the Japan Center, offers Cyber Bowl, with black lights, fog machines, and dance music on Tuesday, Saturday, and Sunday nights. You'll need to make reservations and pool your money; each lane costs $50–$65 for an evening, but that's for up to six people. Cyber bowling isn't exactly an authentic Japanese experience, but it sure is fun.

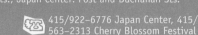 Bounded by Geary Blvd. and Fillmore, Laguna, and Bush Sts.; Japan Center: Post and Buchanan Sts.

 Most shops daily 10–6, Japan Center daily 10–10

 415/922–6776 Japan Center, 415/ 563–2313 Cherry Blossom Festival

 Free

All ages

which runs for a block along Buchanan Street between Sutter and Post streets. More attractive than the Japan Center, it's a pedestrian-only mall with cobbled streets, flowering plum and cherry trees, and several restaurants.

The highlight of the year in Japantown is the Cherry Blossom Festival, held over two weekends each April. Traditional Japanese dancing, often by kids in colorful kimonos, along with fast-paced martial arts demonstrations are presented on an outdoor stage at the Japan Center. There's also a food bazaar and a special Children's Village with arts, crafts, and games. A dazzling 2½-hour parade—running 15 blocks from City Hall to the Japan Center—caps the second weekend. It stars dancers, floats, samurai warriors, *taiko* drummers, shrine bearers, and the festival queen—that's right, not an empress, but all very Japanese.

**TRANSPORTA-TION** Although parking is difficult on the street, the Japan Center has two big indoor parking garages. Most stores, restaurants, the bowling alley, and theaters will validate parking for a specified length of time. Alternately, take Muni's No. 38 Geary bus, which runs between Union Square and the Richmond District and stops at Japantown en route.

**KID-FRIENDLY EATS** Though other types of food *are* available, the idea of going to Japantown and not eating Japanese food is positively un-American. **Mifune** (Kintetsu Bldg., 1737 Post St., Japan Center, tel. 415/922–0337) has tasty, inexpensive noodle dishes, including children's plates. At **Isobune Sushi** (Kintetsu Bldg., 1737 Post St., Japan Center, tel. 415/563–1030), you can pluck the sushi of your choice from little boats as they float around the counter, but make sure your kids eat what they pluck.

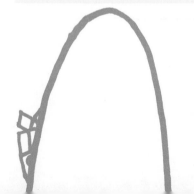

# LAKE MERCED

Until sand dunes cut off its narrow link to the Pacific about a century ago, Lake Merced—in the far southwestern corner of San Francisco—was an ocean-side lagoon. Freshwater has replaced saltwater, and the lake now serves as an emergency city reservoir. But pretty Lake Merced is best known as a recreational mecca, providing some of the best and most accessible fishing, boating, windsurfing, picnicking, bicycling, and jogging in the city. Also along its shores lies one of San Francisco's top public golf courses, heavily forested Harding Park.

The lake has 7 miles of shoreline, bordered much of the way by tule rushes and frequented by migratory birds. A moderately level path that's a favorite of cyclists, joggers, and walkers loops around the lake. The path is partly shaded by eucalyptus, cypress, and pine trees; wildflowers, ferns, and berry bushes also line the route at points.

A narrow isthmus cuts the lake almost in two. The southern portion is larger and more popular for boating, and you can rent rowboats, paddleboats, canoes, kayaks, and boats

**KEEP IN MIND** While you can park in one of several lots around the lake to access the pathway that loops around it, the best place to park for fishing and boating is near the Boathouse, on Harding Park Road off Skyline Boulevard. And remember that because the lake is near the coast, it's often foggy, misty, and cool here. (Summer is actually one of the coolest and foggiest seasons.) Dress accordingly.

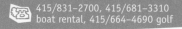 Sloat, Skyline, Lake Merced, and Sunset Blvds.

415/831–2700, 415/681–3310
boat rental, 415/664–4690 golf

 Free

 Daily 24 hrs, boat rental 6:30–sunset

All ages

with electric motors or take sailing lessons from the Lake Merced Boating and Fishing Company. (Rowboats, the cheapest, are $9 per hour, $25 for a full day.) Fishing is more common along the northern and western shores of the lake, whose waters are stocked with trout—in fact, it's one of the top spots for lake fishing in the Bay Area. As you might guess from its name, the Lake Merced Boating and Fishing Company also rents rods and reels ($8 per day) and other fishing equipment. Windsurfing lessons have been given here in the past as well, though at press time the lake was seeking a new concessionaire.

So with the exception of swimming and gas-powered motorboating (this is a potential reservoir after all), if there's an activity your family finds fun on or around still water, you can probably find it here.

**KID-FRIENDLY EATS** The **Boathouse** (1 Harding Park Rd., tel. 415/681–2727), on the road to the golf course and surrounded on two sides by lake, has a sports-bar atmosphere and can get rowdy on football Sundays. Nevertheless, it serves kid-friendly food like hot dogs and chicken nuggets. Not far away, **Leon's Bar-B-Q** (*see* Ft. Funston) dishes up ribs and jambalaya. Picnic tables are situated around the lake—many in a grassy area near the Boathouse—and the boat-rental concession sells snacks.

# LAWRENCE HALL OF SCIENCE

Follow signs up the hill from Gayley Road on the eastern end of the University of California campus to the Lawrence Hall of Science—a memorial to Ernest O. Lawrence, the university's first Nobel laureate and an inventor of the atomic bomb. The museum is loaded with interactive exhibits geared mostly toward children, which can entertain them for hours. Big hands-on displays and flashy special exhibitions are typical here. The emphasis is on biology, chemistry, and astronomy.

Once you've found this museum nestled up a winding road high in the Berkeley hills, linger in the outer courtyard to let your children clamber over the 60-foot-long model of DNA, while you enjoy panoramic views of San Francisco Bay. Or take a short walk up the nearby hillside to find the wind organ, a set of 36 long, slender pipes sticking out of the ground; you and your kids will hear music if you walk among them when the wind is blowing. You can also play with their tones by turning one of six moveable pipes.

KEEP IN MIND On clear Saturday evenings from 8 to 11, astronomers bring their telescopes to the Lawrence Hall of Science to give interested visitors a free peek at the moon, planets, star clusters, and galaxies. You can also bring a good pair of binoculars for your own use. Call the hall and select the astronomy information option for tips on what constellations, eclipses, and such you can see in the sky on a particular night.

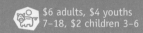

Inside, permanent exhibitions include Math Rules!—a collection of puzzles and hands-on challenges to show kids that math doesn't have to be dull—and Within the Human Brain, which demonstrates how the brain works. (You can even watch a video of a human brain dissection.) The Earthquakes exhibit contains a working seismograph and tips on surviving the Big One. Just Build It allows budding young architects to construct with building blocks.

The museum also hosts periodic Fun Day events—from making music with math and science to studying the behavior and lore of whales—and special temporary exhibitions. Call for an upcoming schedule. On weekends, holidays, and three times daily in summer, you can attend a show at the Holt Planetarium. Films, lectures, and laboratory demonstrations are also offered weekends, daily in summer.

**HEY, KIDS!** How would you like to pet a snake or hold a tarantula? In the Biology Discovery Lab, you can do just that on weekends, holidays, and every day in summer. The museum also has open computer labs on weekends, in case the closest you want to get to a snake and its food is a "mouse."

**KID-FRIENDLY EATS** The museum's **Small Planet Café** (tel. 510/ 644–1880) serves hot dogs, soups, sandwiches, and salads. You can also picnic at nearby Tilden Park (*see below*), or drive back down out of the hills to eat at **Fat Apple's** (1346 Martin Luther King Jr. Blvd., tel. 510/526–2260), where the burgers always draw big crowds. For kids with more adventurous tastes, try **Cha Am** (1543 Shattuck Ave., tel. 510/848– 9664), where pad Thai and other tasty Thai dishes are served at bargain prices.

# LIBERTY SHIP JEREMIAH O'BRIEN

During World War II, some two-thirds of America's fleet of more than 2,700 Liberty Ships were built in the Bay Area. (The Liberty Ships were part of a merchant fleet designed to carry wartime supplies and troops across the Atlantic.) Ironically, the U.S.S. *Jeremiah O'Brien* was built in Oregon. But more than a half century later, the *Jeremiah O'Brien*—the only one of the Liberty Ships to remain afloat and in its original condition—is now integrally associated with San Francisco, berthed most of the year at Pier 32 along the waterfront south of the Bay Bridge, and in summer at Pier 45 at Fisherman's Wharf.

The city, and the entire area, embraced the gray-hulled ship and its history when, in 1994, it was restored and sailed by volunteers across the Atlantic to mark the 50th anniversary of the D-Day invasion in Normandy, to which it had ferried troops. In fact, it was the only U.S. vessel to both take part in the invasion and return for the anniversary. Most of the Liberty Ships were sold off after World War II or scrapped after Vietnam; about 200 were sunk during the second world war.

**KEEP IN MIND** The ship usually makes cruises on the bay twice a year: around Memorial Day and during Fleet Week in October. You can come aboard for $100 a person (same price for adults and kids). Cruises run 9–4ish, and a light breakfast and buffet lunch are served. Call for reservations.

**HEY, KIDS!** Try to guess how long it took to build this massive ship. If you guessed "just under two months," you'd be right. One Liberty Ship was built in just four days, and many were built in less than a month. They were needed, quickly, for the war effort in Europe, and speed was considered more essential than long-term durability. That may be why the *Jeremiah O'Brien* is the only one still afloat.

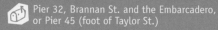 Pier 32, Brannan St. and the Embarcadero, or Pier 45 (foot of Taylor St.)

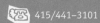 415/441-3101

 $5 adults, $3 children 6–18

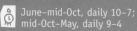 June–mid-Oct, daily 10–7; mid-Oct–May, daily 9–4

 6 and up

Today, the entire ship—which is 441 feet long and whose gross weight is 7,176 tons—maintains its 1940s appearance. You and your children can walk the decks, where antiaircraft guns (no longer loaded, of course) remain on vigil, and then go below to explore the mazelike corridors, the sailors' quarters, the radio operator's room, and the bridge.

For a really claustrophobic experience, descend to the lower level of the vessel and into the depths of the boiler room, where the enormous engines are still in working order. They have to be, since the *Jeremiah O'Brien* still makes periodic cruises on the bay, which you can take part in if the timing (and the money) is right.

**KID-FRIENDLY EATS** The most convenient restaurant is right across the Embarcadero from Pier 32. **Delancey Street** (600 Embarcadero, at Brannan St., tel. 415/512–5179) has American standards like burgers, sandwiches, and salads, and there's some patio seating. The food tends to be a bit better one block south, however, at **Town's End Restaurant and Bakery** (2 Townsend St., tel. 415/512–0749), whose specialties are great breakfasts and delicious baked goods. For more eateries *see* Fisherman's Wharf.

# LINDSAY WILDLIFE MUSEUM

The centerpiece of this East Bay museum, founded in 1955, is the nation's oldest and one of its largest wildlife rehabilitation centers. The Lindsay treats more than 6,000 injured or orphaned animals each year, representing 200 different species mostly native to California—among them bald eagles, hawks, vultures, owls, mountain lions, bobcats, coyotes, foxes, snakes, roadrunners, and rabbits. A bald eagle, for instance, may have become entangled in a power line. A hawk may have crashed into a home's window. An owl may have flown into the path of a car. Wildlife officers bring them in, as do hikers and homeowners. Nearly half are eventually returned to the wild. Those creatures too sick, injured, or tame to survive on their own may be put on display at the museum—a sparkling facility that was expanded and remodeled in 1994.

Don't think of the Lindsay as a zoo, though. Its goal is not to show off the animals but to teach the public about California wildlife, the impact of human activity on it, and how the needs of people can be balanced with those of wild animals. Daily presentations allow closer

**HEY, KIDS!** The museum's Pet Library Program lets you check out a live domestic (not wild) rabbit, guinea pig, hamster, or rat for one week. These animals were once pets, but their former families couldn't keep them. It's a good way to find out if you're ready to have a pet full-time yourself or, if you can't, to just enjoy caring for one temporarily. Have your parents call the museum for more information, and bring one of them along when you go.

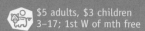

looks at certain animals, and you can watch as some are fed. But there's nothing flashy or cute here: The animals don't do tricks, there's no petting of wild creatures, and staff members don't pretend that the animals want to be here. Birds and mammals on display for three months are given three months off to reduce the stresses of being watched by all those human visitors. (During these "vacations," museum employees or volunteers take the animals home with them.)

A number of exhibits are geared toward young children. In the Discovery Room, your youngsters can explore a 10-foot by 10-foot scale model of a backyard that may be similar to your own. There they can hunt for animals—an opossum, a squirrel, a screech owl, a bat, a raccoon—that are making themselves at home there. (These animals aren't alive, though—they've visited the taxidermist.)

**KID-FRIENDLY EATS** No food services are nearby, but Larkey Park does have picnic tables. Downtown Walnut Creek has many family-style places. For good sandwiches and kids' menus, visit **Max's Opera Café** (1676 N. California Blvd., tel. 925/932–3434). **High Tech Burrito** (1815 Ignacio Valley Rd., tel. 925/938–3888) is a local branch of a reliable burrito/taco minichain.

**KEEP IN MIND** If a visit to the museum only whets your children's animal appetite, they (and you) can choose from a wide variety of classes for kids (as young as 2) and families. Live animals are used in classes, where appropriate. Two one-week animal-oriented summer camps are available for children 6–10. One week explores the ways animals sense the world, another the way animals adapt to it. Some camp sessions are held in Larkey Park.

# LOMBARD STREET

Officially, it's the 1000 block of Lombard Street, but everybody knows it as "the Crookedest Street in the World." (The end of Vermont Street on Potrero Hill may actually be *more* crooked, but it's way off the beaten path.) Lombard's eight hairpin curves, which zigzag down the east face of Russian Hill, are some of the most heavily driven, and photographed, stretches of roadway in existence.

To best appreciate Lombard Street, you'll need a car, and then a parking space (the latter can present a problem). At the intersection of Hyde and Lombard—where you may well encounter a mini-traffic jam—begin your snake-like journey down the red-cobblestone-lined street. It's impossible, really, to take it anything but slow or (for the driver) to do anything but steer back and forth. Kids usually love the ride. Have them count the curves as you go down, and to make it a real surprise, don't tell them where they're going before starting down. Chances are your car will show up in countless other people's photographs as you'll probably see scads of picture-snapping tourists both at the beginning and the end of the block.

**TRANSPORTATION** Don't try this drive with an RV or any extra-long vehicle. If you don't have a car at all, you can ride a Powell–Hyde cable car to Lombard Street (ask the conductor to call out the nearest stop). The street is well worth seeing even if you can't drive it.

**HEY, KIDS!** If you want to ride down another of San Francisco's steepest streets, ask your parents to take you to Filbert Street between Hyde and Leavenworth—just two blocks from the Crookedest Street. This one has a 31.5% grade but no switchbacks. It's just straight down, and when you start down (you can't drive up), you can't see where you're headed. Your mom or dad will want to take it slow. Before the zigzag road was built, Lombard Street was even steeper.

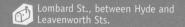
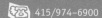

Once you've completed the driving portion and found a parking space up the street somewhere, you're ready to get a more leisurely view as a pedestrian. You can walk straight up or down the street—steps line either side of it—or just position yourself at the top or bottom for a view of the procession of cars. If your kids have their own cameras, they'll no doubt want to join the picture-taking.

The crooked street—designed in the 1920s to enable drivers to negotiate the 40% grade— is beautifully landscaped with flowers, shrubs, and other plants and lined on either side with houses, whose occupants must feel they're living in a fishbowl without the water.

**KID-FRIENDLY EATS** **Pete's Café** (800 Chestnut St., tel. 415/749–4567) serves the students at the San Francisco Art Institute, but the public is welcome, too. The salads are fresh, the sandwiches good, and the bay views are terrific, all at bargain prices. **Zarzuela** (2000 Hyde St., tel. 415/346– 0800) serves some of the best tapas—Spanish-style appetizer plates—in the city. The portions are perfect for kids, and service is friendly.

# MAKE*A*CIRCUS

Ladies and gentlemen, boys and girls, step right up. You, too, can be a circus star, thanks to the amazing, death-defying Make*A*Circus—well, okay, maybe not death-defying, but certainly entertaining. This San Francisco–based nonprofit group has been presenting free circus festivals in public parks, recreation centers, school yards, and other outdoor spaces around the Bay Area every summer for more than a quarter-century. As each three-part show unfolds, your children get to watch a one-ring circus, learn how to perform, and then take the stage themselves—all in about three hours.

First comes a fast-paced production of original circus theater, staged by the performers of Make*A*Circus. These musical plays typically include daring aerial and acrobatic stunts, juggling, clowns, and jazzy music. Next, in a series of 45-minute circus-arts workshops, audience members from toddlers to teens are invited to learn some basics of clowning, juggling, tumbling, and building human pyramids. All kids are welcome—there's even a workshop for children under 5, who learn dance and song. The grand finale, which presents the conclusion to the

**HEY, KIDS!** If you're aged 14–19 and enrolled in school, you may be able to attend the Make*A*Circus Teen Apprentice Program, in which you can learn juggling, acrobatics, stilt-walking, face-painting, and clowning. You might also be chosen to take part in Make*A*Circus productions as a paid summer apprentice. Classes are free and held in San Francisco in winter.

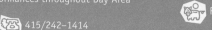
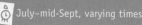

unfinished show, lets those same kids show off their new skills for their families, friends, and the rest of the audience—who usually whoop and holler with delight at the high-energy antics.

Each summer's show has a new theme, often combining fantasy and fable with easy-to-absorb messages about social issues, such as racial intolerance or the dangers of second-hand smoke. In one recent production, for instance, kids became superheroes, traveling down a giant windpipe into a pair of lungs, where they battled the smoke demons, Tar and Nicotine; meanwhile, a pumping heart was personified by a trapeze artist. The story lines aren't preachy, though; they're too much fun for that.

Besides various San Francisco locations, look for summer Make*A*Circus performances in other communities. Call for a schedule.

**KID-FRIENDLY EATS** Except for a few special shows, such as each summer's opening day performance, Make*A*Circus does not have food concessions available. You might want to carry some snacks with you. (After all, what would a circus be without popcorn or peanuts?) For restaurants, *see* listings for those attractions nearest the Make*A*Circus performance you attend.

**KEEP IN MIND** As part of its Clown Therapy Program, Make*A*Circus teaches classes in clowning and circus skills to physically, mentally, and emotionally disabled kids. If appropriate, the kids get to showcase their new skills to audiences of family and friends at the end. Call for more information.

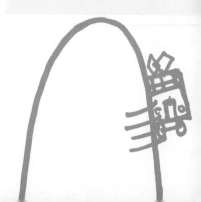

# MARINA GREEN

The Marina Green is one of San Francisco's prettiest parks. Running the equivalent of eight city blocks, it's a wide stretch of grass and bay-side walkways that's popular with kite-flyers, joggers, in-line skaters, bicyclists, jugglers, sunbathers, picnickers, and touch-football and volleyball players. It's just steps away from the beach at Crissy Field, which is part of the Presidio (*see below*), and borders the Marina Small Craft Harbor, where hundreds of pleasure boats are docked. Its western end is across from one of the country's top family museums, the Exploratorium (*see above*). If you're walking the gorgeous 3½-mile Golden Gate Promenade, a paved trail that runs from Aquatic Park to the Golden Gate Bridge, you'll pass by here. Wherever you're heading, linger awhile; benches look out toward Alcatraz and the Golden Gate Bridge, and there's plenty of grass for stretching out.

This is one of San Francisco's top spots for kite-flying. On weekends you may see dozens of colorful, elaborate kites—some shaped like dragons, butterflies, or other exotic creatures—with long tails flapping in the breezes. Big flat expanses and a regular breeze off the

**KID-FRIENDLY EATS** This is a terrific spot for spreading a picnic lunch out on the grass. Or visit **Greens** (*see the Farallon National Wildlife Refuge*), a vegetarian restaurant at Ft. Mason, or **Café Marimba** (*see the Exploratorium*) for Mexican food.

**KEEP IN MIND** Just east of the Marina Green sits Ft. Mason Center (tel. 415/441–3400 or 415/979–3010 events), a former military post that's now a cultural center containing the Young Performers Theatre (tel. 415/346–5550), where kids are the stars; offices of the Golden Gate National Recreation Area (tel. 415/556–0560); and three museums: the Museo Italo Americano (tel. 415/673–2200), the San Francisco Craft and Folk Art Museum (tel. 415/775–0990), and the Mexican Museum (tel. 415/441–0404), which will be moving near Yerba Buena Gardens in late 2000.

 Marina Blvd. between Baker and
Buchanan Sts.

 415/831-2700

 Free

 Daily 24 hrs

All ages

bay usually make flying good for everyone, but occasional tricky winds call for more expert flyers.

With a small detour, you can catch one of San Francisco's most unusual—and overlooked—attractions, which is at the eastern tip of the breakwater that forms the Marina Small Craft Harbor. Start on the western end of the Marina Green (at the foot of Baker Street); then follow the path past the St. Francis Yacht Club east to the Wave Organ. Here "natural music" is made by waves as they funnel through some 20 granite pipes. Come at high tide for the best effect. Your kids can climb on the rocks while you relax on the stone steps and enjoy the "concert" along with views of yachts and the bay.

HEY, KIDS! From Marina Green, face south (away from the water) and look toward the neatly kept houses lining Marina Boulevard. Imagine that you're standing here in October 1989, when a powerful earthquake severely damaged the Marina District. Many houses, streets, and sidewalks crumbled from the enormous waves of energy that traveled all the way from Santa Cruz, 75 miles south. The area is built on landfill—mostly sand. If you've ever built a sand castle, you know how unsteady sand can be.

# MARIN HEADLANDS

Just across the Golden Gate Bridge from San Francisco, the Marin Headlands occupy 12,000 acres of rolling coastal hills from East Ft. Baker to the rocky Pacific shores. They're yet another part of the vast Golden Gate National Recreation Area and best known for their signature views: panoramas of the San Francisco skyline as seen through the bridge's soaring orange cables. Your kids will probably recognize these fabulous bird's-eye views from countless TV commercials, and if you can time your drive so that fog is beginning to roll through—but doesn't completely obscure—the bridge, you'll have struck picture-postcard gold.

The headlands contain over 100 miles of paved roads, unpaved fire roads, and foot, mountain-bike, and horse trails, but most people's introduction is via scenic Conzelman Road. Accessible from the northern end of the bridge, Conzelman Road hugs the cliffs for 5 miles to Point Bonita, where a ½-mile hike leads to the 1855-vintage Point Bonita Lighthouse.

**HEY, KIDS!** Ask your parents if you can stop at the free Marine Mammal Center (tel. 415/289–7325), open daily 10–4. This rescue and rehab center for sick, injured, or orphaned sea lions, seals, sea otters, whales, and porpoises is one of the world's largest wildlife hospitals. Here you can learn about ocean life, hear how marine biologists have rescued whales stranded on nearby beaches, and actually see some recuperating animals, perhaps seal pups being bottle-fed by volunteers.

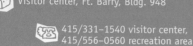 Visitor center, Ft. Barry, Bldg. 948

415/331–1540 visitor center,
415/556–0560 recreation area

 Free

 Visitor center daily 9:30–4:30; lighthouse
Sa–M 12:30–3:30

3 and up

Along the way, you may want to stop and explore some old military fortifications and gun batteries. The tunnels and bunkers, which date back to the 1870s, were constructed to help guard the Golden Gate from foreign attack. Battery 129, located at Hawk Hill along Conzelman Road, provides unobstructed 360° views of the bridge, the city, and the bay. Kids often enjoy crawling through its tunnels, originally designed for cannons. Many of the old forts have now been put to peaceful uses. Ft. Baker, at the foot of the bridge, now houses the Bay Area Discovery Museum (*see above*). Several miles west, Ft. Barry's onetime chapel has been converted to the Marin Headlands Visitors Center, which has displays on natural history and serves as the starting point for ranger-led walks. Not far away, at Ft. Cronkhite, is a marine mammal rehabilitation center, and not far away from that, Rodeo Lagoon is populated with loons, grebes, and other birds. Rodeo Beach lies just beyond. It all adds up to a lot of natural beauty in this part of San Francisco's backyard.

KID-FRIENDLY EATS There are no restaurants in the Marin Headlands, so bring a picnic lunch and find a hillside or beach with a view. For restaurants in nearby Sausalito, *see* the Bay Area Discovery Museum and the Bay Model Visitor Center.

KEEP IN MIND If you want to explore the old fortifications along Conzelman Road, be sure to bring flashlights and old clothes for crawling through the tunnels. And if you're interested in exploring the Marin Headlands at greater length—perhaps doing some camping or hiking here—call the visitor center or the Golden Gate National Recreation Area for information, directions, and trail conditions.

# M.H. DE YOUNG MEMORIAL MUSEUM

A cross from the California Academy of Sciences in Golden Gate Park, the de Young probably has the best collection of American art on the West Coast: an array of paintings, sculpture, and decorative arts that dates from Colonial times to the 20th century. Among the more than 200 paintings by American masters, your kids might particularly enjoy Frederic Church's *Rainy Season in the Tropics,* a landscape with a colorful rainbow; Thomas Moran's landscapes of the Grand Canyon of the Yellowstone; the trompe l'oeil artworks of William Harnett; and works by James Whistler, Grant Wood, and Mary Cassatt. Your children might also take to collections of paintings, sculpture, textiles, baskets, and ceramics from Africa, Oceania, and the Americas. The de Young also hosts traveling blockbuster exhibitions from around the world.

The museum reaches out to families and children in several ways, starting with Gallery One, a year-round art area that exhibits works from the permanent collections enhanced by printed family guides called "Do You See What I See?" Gallery One also has drop-in art

## HEY, KIDS!
Check out the Old West paintings by Albert Bierstadt. *California Spring* and *View of Donner Lake* are set in the Golden State. *Indian Hunting Buffalo* gave people back East a misleading impression of Native Americans. How does it differ from what you know?

**KEEP IN MIND** Don't overlook the Asian Art Museum of San Francisco (tel. 415/379–8801) while it remains in its home adjoining the de Young; it's a bonus offered at no extra charge. The West Coast's largest museum of Asian art, it showcases art spanning 6,000 years from more than 40 countries and contains nearly 12,000 sculptures, paintings, and ceramics—almost overwhelming for kids. But intricately carved jade, colorful porcelains, ceramic and bronze animal figures, and a large collection of Japanese inro (small lacquer boxes for carrying personal items) should spark their interest.

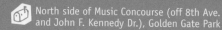
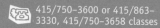
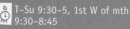

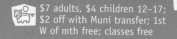

North side of Music Concourse (off 8th Ave. and John F. Kennedy Dr.), Golden Gate Park

415/750-3600 or 415/863-3330, 415/750-3658 classes

$7 adults, $4 children 12–17; $2 off with Muni transfer; 1st W of mth free; classes free

T–Su 9:30–5, 1st W of mth 9:30–8:45

3 and up, classes 3–12

workshops for families, a reading area with children's art books, writing and drawing tables, and a computer station with access to arts collections. On most Saturday mornings, the museum also sponsors art classes for kids in Hearst Court. Classes include gallery tours, and no preregistration is necessary. As at the California Palace of the Legion of Honor (*see above*), your kids, depending on their ages, can take Doing and Viewing Art or Big Kids, Little Kids.

The de Young is San Francisco's oldest public museum, dating from 1894, and its eight buildings are something of a hodgepodge and not up to earthquake code. Beginning around 2001 and extending to the year 2006 or so, the de Young will undergo a complete renovation, so watch for major changes during that time. The adjoining Asian Art Museum of San Francisco is moving downtown to the old Main Library building in the Civic Center in late 2001, and the de Young will use that space for temporary exhibitions during the renovations.

**KID-FRIENDLY EATS Café de Young** (tel. 415/752–0116), located in a garden setting on the ground floor of the museum, overlooks a small pool with flowers and has umbrella-topped tables. The menu has salads and sandwiches, and kids can get a half sandwich with soup. The **Teahouse** (*see* Golden Gate Park), in the Japanese Tea Garden next to the De Young, specializes in tea and cookies. *See* the California Academy of Sciences for other good restaurants nearby.

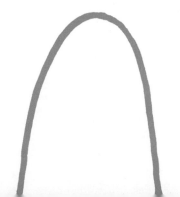

# MISSION CLIFFS

To get your family psyched for tackling the granite cliffs or massive boulders of Yosemite and Joshua Tree national parks—or at least that big rock in your backyard—head to San Francisco's only indoor rock-climbing gym, one of the largest in the Bay Area. Located within a giant former warehouse in the Mission District, Mission Cliffs offers some 14,000 square feet of artificial climbing terrain. A weight room, saunas, lockers, showers, and pro shop are also on the premises.

Kids climb brown walls studded with foot and hand holds and are secured by harness and rope to the ceiling or the top of the wall. Your kids can come for fun to try it out, or even just to watch, but if they like it—and most kids do—they can sign up for classes.

The Kids Belay classes are a good way to introduce your kids to the sport. ("Belay" means securing the rope for a rock climber.) Classes are available on a drop-in basis all day on weekends. Instruction not only teaches your children about climbing but also, in the process, should help them develop

HEY, KIDS! If you get bitten by the climbing bug, why not check out (or ask your parents to check out) the other offerings available to kids here? (You'll want to run the prices by your folks before getting too carried away.) These include parties ($100 for five children, $18 each additional child), after-school camps ($200 for 10 weeks on Wednesday afternoons), and summer camps ($150–$200 for a week of mornings, including time outdoors).

 2295 Harrison St.

 415/550-0515

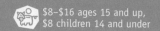 $8–$16 ages 15 and up,
$8 children 14 and under

 M, W, and F 6:30 AM–10 PM; T and Th
11–10; Sa–Su 10–6

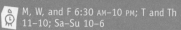 4 and up

balance, coordination, concentration, and self-confidence. Though the atmosphere is informal and fun, supervision is close, with a ratio of one staff member to every six kids. Meanwhile, you can watch and relax, use the weight room free of charge, or learn how to belay your child yourself by taking a Belay Safety Class. Recommended for first-time climbers, this class demonstrates the proper use of belay equipment, knot tying, and basic top-rope climbing, with an emphasis on safety and personal responsibility. It's offered weekend afternoons. Private climbing lessons are also available, as are memberships, which provide discounts on lessons.

With some lessons under their harness, children learn the basics quickly. Many 7–9 year-olds grasp within a week how to put on a harness, tie a figure-eight knot, belay, and climb a wall. Younger kids generally take longer; and those 10 and up can often pick it up in a lesson or two—perhaps faster than Mom and Dad.

**KID-FRIENDLY EATS** La Taqueria (2889 Mission St., tel. 415/285-7117) has terrific burritos and tacos, fresh fruit drinks, and clean, colorful surroundings. The **St. Francis Fountain and Candy Store** (2801 24th St., tel. 415/826-4200), the city's oldest (1918) and most atmospheric soda fountain, serves basic lunches and dinners along with ice cream treats and candy.

**KEEP IN MIND** Aside from sneakers, your children won't need to bring any particular equipment for the Kids Belay class; harnesses will be provided. Remember, however, that rock climbing does pose physical risk, and everyone participating must sign a release of liability and assumption of risk form (in the case of kids, a parent must sign for them). If you want to belay your own child, you must first pass a staff-administered test.

# MISSION DOLORES

Historic buildings may not be at the top of your kids' "fun things to do" list, but Mission Dolores has some things going for it. For starters, you can tell them it's the oldest building in San Francisco—more than 200 years old, in fact. The mission was completed in 1791, one of a string of 21 Spanish missions in California founded by Father Junipero Serra around the time the United States was gaining independence from England back on the East Coast. To get to be the oldest building, Mission Dolores has had to survive three major earthquakes, including the devastating 1906 quake and fire that almost wiped out the city. (The 4-foot-thick original sun-dried adobe mud walls helped the mission weather all that intense shaking and baking.)

Don't mistake the humble historic mission for the newer (1913), multidomed basilica next door, where most local parishioners come to worship. The old mission is small—the simplest, by design, of the state's historic missions. It's also one of the best preserved. Be sure to look up at the ceiling, where local Costanoans hand-painted Native American designs

**KEEP IN MIND** For the young and the restless, Mission Dolores Park (18th and Dolores Sts.) is two blocks away. Here you'll find lots of green grass for picnicking and sunbathing, tennis and basketball courts, a playground, a dog-run area, and some great views of the city from its hillsides.

**HEY, KIDS!** In the cemetery, see if you can find the burial sites of Don Francisco de Haro and Don Luis Antonio Arguello. De Haro was the first mayor of San Francisco, and Arguello was the first governor of Alta (or "upper") California, back in the days before California was part of the United States. Both have San Francisco streets named after them.

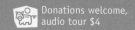

with vegetable dyes. The tiny chapel is decorated with frescoes and a hand-painted wooden altar; some artifacts were brought from Mexico by mule in the late 18th century. A small museum holds other historic pieces. You can rent an audio tour, which contains interesting background information, but it lasts 45 minutes, so it's best suited for older kids.

The old cemetery next to the chapel is the most intriguing sight. Here in the oldest tombs in the city, dozens of early San Francisco pioneers and settlers are buried, including a number of children who died during the Gold Rush days—a poignant reminder of the hardships of those times. Lying in unmarked graves in back are the remains of an estimated 5,000 Native Americans. The cemetery was made famous by a scene in the 1958 Hitchcock film *Vertigo,* in which Kim Novak's character paid a visit here. It's still worth making a trip.

**KID-FRIENDLY EATS** Picnic at Mission Dolores Park, or choose one of the area's inexpensive ethnic restaurants. **La Cumbre Taqueria** (515 Valencia St., tel. 415/863–8205) has some of the best burritos in the city, and the *carne asada* (grilled steak) is tops. **Ti Couz** (3108 16th St., tel. 415/252–7373) specializes in Breton-style crepes, both savory (salmon, mushroom) and sweet (chocolate- or sweet-fruit filled). Frequent lines at both restaurants, reflecting their popularity, are the only downside.

Usually called Mt. Tam, Mt. Tamalpais dominates the skyline in Marin County (rising to 2,571 feet) and is the top hiking and mountain biking spot in the Bay Area. Dozens of trails lead to redwoods, waterfalls, and panoramic views stretching to San Francisco, Marin County, the bay, and the Pacific Ocean. About 50 of Mt. Tam's 200 miles of trails are within the 6,300-acre Mt. Tamalpais State Park, which occupies much of the mountain's western and southern slopes. (Much of the rest of Mt. Tam lies within the boundaries of the Marin Municipal Water District or the Golden Gate National Recreation Area, including Muir Woods National Monument; *see below.*)

Top hikes include the short, easy Verna Dunshee Trail, which loops around East Peak (the highest of Mt. Tam's three peaks); the historic Old Railroad Grade, shared with mountain bikes; the Matt Davis Trail, 6.7 miles one way, which leads across the mountain toward Stinson Beach; the redwood-lined Steep Ravine Trail, which drops 1,100 feet; and the grueling Dipsea Trail, 6.8 miles one way, site of a famous annual footrace. Bikes aren't permitted on foot

**HEY, KIDS!** Mountain bikes were invented in the valleys below Mt. Tam in the early 1970s and first tested on the mountain. Before that, however, the Mill Valley and Mount Tamalpais Scenic Railway (1896–1930)—the "world's crookedest railroad"—ran up and down Mt. Tam's southern slope, chugging up 281 hairpin curves for 8 miles between downtown Mill Valley and the East Peak summit. Today, you can bike or hike the Old Railroad Grade from East Peak to Mill Valley's Blithedale Ridge.

trails, but they are allowed on fire roads, paved roads, and "grades." One of the most challenging mountain bike routes—great for teens—is the 8-mile (one way) Old Railroad Grade up to East Peak, guaranteed to get your heart pumping and lungs burning (or to provide a rush heading downhill).

Families who like to camp can do so at two campgrounds, Pantoll and Steep Ravine. The Pantoll Campground lies between the mountain summit and Muir Woods and has 16 walk-in tent sites ($15–$16 per night), awarded at the Pantoll ranger station on a first-come, first-served basis. The Steep Ravine Environmental Campground, on an ocean bluff south of Stinson Beach, has 10 rustic cabins ($30 a night) and six tent sites ($10–$11). Parking permits and reservations are required year-round.

**KID-FRIENDLY EATS** Picnic tables are available at Rock Spring, Laurel Dell Meadow, and the East Peak Summit, which also has a snack bar. The **Mountain Home Inn** (810 Panoramic Hwy., tel. 415/381–9000) serves breakfast weekends and lunch and dinner Tuesday–Sunday. The **Buckeye Roadhouse** (15 Shoreline Hwy., tel. 415/331–2600) has classic American fare.

**KEEP IN MIND** Weather can play a big role in your enjoyment of Mt. Tam and may vary widely on the mountain itself: It's easy to go from warm sun into cool fog. The southern and western slopes, especially, are often fog-covered from June through August, and the best chance for clear skies and views is in late spring and fall, though winter also produces its share of crystal-clear days. Most rain falls between November and April. Spring wildflower season is at its peak from March until mid-May, and yellow jackets may plague picnic areas in summer.

# MOUNTAIN LAKE PARK

Mountain Lake Park, which borders the southern flanks of the Presidio and is one of the city's nicest neighborhood parks, has a long history—or at least the land it stands on does. Back in 1776, the same year the eastern colonies declared their independence from Great Britain, a Spanish military scouting party arrived at this spot after an arduous nine-month, 900-mile-long trek from what is now Mexico. (If you think driving Highway 1 is slow along the coast, try hoofing it.) Spanish soldiers, led by Captain Juan Bautista de Anza and Father Pedro Font (who both now have city streets named after them), made camp here for two days at what is now Mountain Lake Park. Although they didn't actually establish a settlement, they laid the groundwork for later Spaniards who brought about San Francisco's birth.

Today, Mountain Lake Park is a contoured landscape that includes grassy meadows, shaded walkways, tennis and basketball courts, a batting cage, jogging trails, a parcourse with exercise equipment, and a bi-level playground with swings, slides, climbing structures,

**KEEP IN MIND** Though the lake has a beach, the murky water isn't for swimming—leave that to the waterfowl. Fishing isn't allowed, either. You can bring leashed dogs to most areas (not the playground), but for true doggy heaven, go to the southern section, where dogs can run freely.

**HEY, KIDS!** Sure, you're not going to come to Mountain Lake Park for a history lesson, but since this was the spot where San Francisco was born, see if you can find the rock with the plaque on it, marking the spot where the Spaniard Juan Bautista de Anza and his soldiers made camp way back in 1776. Hint: if you sit down on the rock, you'll have a nice view of the lake.

and sand to land in. There are lots of spots for resting on a bench after a hike through the Presidio or for picnicking on the grass or at a table.

The lake for which the park was named is a 4-acre reservoir, bordered by tule reeds and overhanging willows, that served as the city's water supply during Gold Rush days. Today it's a favorite refuge for ducks and swans—and even the occasional alligator. Well, very occasional. No one knows for sure how one soon-to-be famous little alligator invaded the lake back in 1996, but it caused quite a stir and put Mountain Lake Park on the map, if only for its "15 minutes" of fame. Reporters and even gator hunters imported from Florida descended on the lake to try to capture it, and the gator managed to elude them all for days. Secluded Mountain Lake Park eventually returned to being a relatively anonymous—and peaceful—corner of the city.

KID-FRIENDLY EATS Have a picnic in the park, or head to nearby Clement Street for inexpensive Asian food. **Pho Tu Do** (1000 Clement St., tel. 415/221–7111) specializes in reasonably priced, delicious Vietnamese soups; try the beef noodle. **Coriya Hot Pot City** (852 Clement St., tel. 415/387–7888) is an all-you-can-eat Taiwanese place where you cook your own seafood, meat, and vegetables in a hot pot and barbecue. It gets crowded, so come early for dinner.

# MUIR WOODS NATIONAL MONUMENT

Snuggled in a cool, often foggy redwood-lined canyon on the southeastern lower slopes of Mt. Tamalpais, just 12 miles north of the Golden Gate Bridge, Muir Woods National Monument is the world's most famous stand of old-growth redwoods—the last remnants of soaring trees that once covered the mountain and many parts of the Bay Area. As California's most-visited redwood park, this is definitely nature for the masses: The main hiking trails are paved, and the woods are a regular stop on tour bus excursions. But the virgin redwoods—accented with green ferns and colorful azaleas, the scents of moss and bay, and the sounds of splashing Redwood Creek—are so majestic that tranquillity still seems to prevail.

You won't find the tallest redwoods here—those are farther north—but the trees in Muir Woods are up to 250 feet tall. Many were already growing in the days of the Crusades.

Six miles of trails lie fully within the 560-acre park itself. Trails along the canyon floor are mostly level and suited for strollers, and four bridges spanning Redwood Creek allow you to

**HEY, KIDS!** Where there's flora—especially flora the size of these redwoods—there's usually fauna, so keep your eyes peeled for all sorts of wildlife. Salmon spawn in winter and spring; summertime steelhead trout do their thing in Redwood Creek. On land, you may spot black-tailed deer, squirrels, chipmunks, and banana slugs. In fall, look for migrating monarch butterflies and swarms of ladybugs.

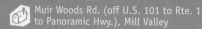

make short loops. The tallest trees in the park are found along the Main Trail in Bohemian Grove (a ½-mile loop from the parking lot) and in Cathedral Grove (a 1-mile loop). Venture just a bit farther, along the unpaved trails—such as the Ben Johnson Trail (2½ miles round-trip)—that lead up out of the canyon into Mt. Tamalpais State Park (*see above*), and you'll be surprised at how few other folks you'll meet.

Muir Woods was named after conservationist John Muir, founder of the Sierra Club, who called this "the best tree lover's monument that could be found in all the forests of the world."

**KID-FRIENDLY EATS** A **snack bar** near the visitor center serves burgers, hot dogs, and apple pie. Picnicking isn't permitted in Muir Woods but is allowed in adjacent Mt. Tamalpais State Park. For information on picnicking and restaurants in the area, refer to the Mt. Tamalpais State Park listing.

**KEEP IN MIND** A few tips can help avoid disappointment or discomfort while visiting Muir Woods: Arrive by midmorning or in late afternoon to avoid the crush of visitors, and go midweek if possible. (Parking lots, including the overflow lots, often fill up by late morning.) Bring jackets or sweatshirts; redwoods flourish in cool, foggy climates, and this is one of them. Watch for poison oak and stinging nettles just off the trails, or better yet, stay on the trails. Although camping is prohibited here, you can camp in adjacent Mt. Tamalpais State Park.

# MURALS OF THE MISSION DISTRICT

They're some of the city's least-known artistic treasures—possibly more famous in Europe than in San Francisco—and you don't need to visit a museum to see them. All you have to do is take a walk (or a bike ride or a drive). Hundreds of outdoor murals decorate the Mission District, and their often brilliant colors and bold subjects can captivate kids just as much as adults.

The first—and still best-known—group of murals is in little Balmy Alley (24th to 25th St., between Harrison and Treat Sts.). Back in the early 1970s, community artists—both adults and children, working alone or in groups—started to adorn the block-long byway's walls with murals featuring such themes as peace in Central America, Latino heritage, and neighborhood pride. (The Mission District is heavily Hispanic.) Since then, dozens more muralists have joined in, so that today much of the street, including walls, fences, and garage doors, is covered with artwork.

**KID-FRIENDLY EATS** You can pick up a snack along 24th Street. After the tour, visit the **St. Francis Fountain and Candy Store** (see Mission Cliffs). **Roosevelt Tamale Parlor** (2817 24th St., tel. 415/550–9213) has been dishing up Tex-Mex classics since 1922.

**KEEP IN MIND** For any walk, whether guided or self- guided, wear comfortable shoes, and carry snacks and water. And, of course, before you set out on a tour, make sure your child is old enough to walk for up to two hours and possibly sit through a ½-hour slide show. In addition to the tours conducted through the Precita Eyes Mural Arts and Visitors Center, there are other, less frequent (but free) walking tours of the Mission murals offered by City Guides (tel. 415/557–4266). These tours are given on selected Saturdays, so it's best to call for a schedule.

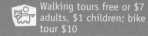  

Balmy Alley, Mission District; mural center, 2981 24th St.; bike tours from 348 Precita Ave.

415/285-2287 mural center

Walking tours free or $7 adults, $1 children; bike tour $10

Walking tours Sa–Su 1:30 or by appt; bike tours 2nd Su of mth at 11

4 and up

Like those in Balmy Alley, most Mission District murals are in the area bordered on the west by Mission Street, the east by Potrero Avenue, the north by 20th Street, and the south by Precita Avenue, next to Precita Park. Down the block from Balmy Alley, Precita Eyes Mural Arts and Visitors Center sells Mission mural walk maps for $1.50.

You can also take a guided walking or bike tour. The mural center leads the most frequent walking tours, which last about two hours and cover an eight-block area with 75–90 murals. Drop-in tours are given on weekend afternoons; call for reservations for other days. A ½-hour slide show on the making of murals precedes the afternoon tours. The tour guides—muralists themselves—are attuned to the needs of kids. Bike tours, for any age person who can ride (bring bike and helmet), take in more than 100 murals.

**HEY, KIDS!** Though it's hard to pick out specific murals among all those in Balmy Alley, look for one called "Indigenous Eyes: War and Peace." (It's on a garage door about halfway down the alley.) And yes, the skeleton and dove in each eye stand for war and peace. It depicts life in Central America during years of civil war and unrest. Another colorful mural shows a San Francisco bus, tropical birds, monkeys, and little children. What do you think it's trying to say?

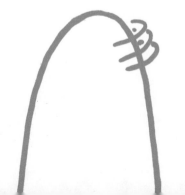

# NOB HILL

Nob Hill has been one of the city's most prestigious addresses since the late 19th century, when railroad magnates and Comstock Lode silver barons built the most expensive homes California had ever seen. All but one of the houses were destroyed in the earthquake of 1906, and the lone survivor, the brownstone Flood Mansion, is now the exclusive Pacific Union Club. But the legacy of the railroad magnates—Charles Crocker, Mark Hopkins, Collis P. Huntington, and Leland Stanford (known as the Big Four)—and other tycoons lives on in the luxury apartment buildings and hotels (including the Mark Hopkins, Huntington, and Fairmont) that line this high-rent hill. It rises steeply above Chinatown and the Financial District to a height of 376 feet.

To rub elbows with the wealthy or, at least, their dogs, kids, and nannies, take a break at the top of the hill in Huntington Park. Find a spot on a bench in this neat, tidy park while your kids take to the swings, the slide, and the climbing structures on the sand-based playground. This is a dog-friendly park; chances are at least one pooch will be chasing a Frisbee while

HEY, KIDS! Wonder how Nob Hill got its name? Nob came from "nabob," a term used in colonial India for a man of wealth or importance. Once, the area was simply called California Street Hill. After the cable car arrived in 1873, however, it became easier to scale the hill from the Financial District, and many of the richest San Franciscans—the local "nabobs"—moved up here.

California, Taylor, Sacramento, and Mason Sts.; Grace Cathedral, Taylor and California Sts.

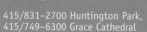
415/831–2700 Huntington Park, 415/749–6300 Grace Cathedral

Free

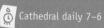
Cathedral daily 7–6

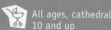
All ages, cathedral 10 and up

others are chasing each other. (Owners are warned to keep them out of the children's play area, however.) Watch for expensive pedigrees—after all, this *is* Nob Hill.

The park sits across from Grace Cathedral, modeled after Notre Dame in Paris. The Episcopal cathedral has a 15th-century French altarpiece, luminous stained-glass windows, and gilded-bronze doors similar to those at the Baptistry in Florence, Italy. So visiting here is like taking the kids on a mini-trip to Europe. Don't overlook the cathedral's intriguing indoor and outdoor labyrinths, based on one at France's Chartres Cathedral. Each labyrinth forms a long, meandering path that leads in a geometric pattern to the center of a circle and back out again, representing an interfaith path of prayer and meditation. Though many children like to walk the labyrinths, they should respect others following the paths, remain peaceful, and not use them for racing.

**KID-FRIENDLY EATS** The **Nob Hill Café** (1152 Taylor St., tel. 415/776–6500) dishes up pastas, pizza, and chocolaty desserts in friendly surroundings. Don't confuse it with the **Nob Hill Noshery Café** (1400 Pacific Ave., tel. 415/928–6674), which serves breakfast, lunch, and dinner. Best bets are the deli-style sandwiches.

**TRANSPORTATION** The best way to get to Nob Hill is to ride the California Street cable car line to the top. The ride is steep and as much fun as many theme park rides for kids. You can board the cable car anywhere along California Street between Van Ness Avenue and the foot of Market Street. Rides cost $2 each for anyone 6 or older; little ones are free. If you do decide to drive, note that street parking is tight, and parking garages are expensive.

# OAKLAND MUSEUM OF CALIFORNIA

Maybe because it's across San Francisco Bay in Oakland, this attractive, innovative museum on the south shore of Lake Merritt doesn't get the recognition it deserves. Its architecture alone—three tiers of galleries with gardens, courts, terraces, lawns, and pond in a complex covering four square blocks—makes it well worth a stop. But if you want to get a sense of California's history, environment, art, and diversity, this museum is a must.

In the Cowell Hall of California History, for example, your kids can whisk their imaginations back to the days of Native Americans, missions and ranchos, the Gold Rush, the Victorian era, and 1960s-era California—captured in the film *American Graffiti* and in the spirit of San Francisco's Summer of Love—right up to the current-day technology of Silicon Valley. In the Hall of California Ecology, your family can take a simulated walk across the state—from the coast to the Sierra to the desert—to view the terrain, vegetation, and wildlife as it looked before the arrival of Europeans. In the Aquatic California Gallery, you can get an overview of the state's ocean, river, stream, and estuary environments. And in the Gallery of California

**KEEP IN MIND** Relax with a boat ride on Lake Merritt (*see* Children's Fairyland) after the museum. You can rent rowboats, canoes, paddleboats, or small sailboats from the Lake Merritt Boating Center (tel. 510/444–3807). Lakeside Park also has playgrounds, gardens, and picnic spots.

**HEY, KIDS!** In the Cowell Hall of California History, watch for the three interactive History Information Stations: touch-screen computers that give further information about the things you see on display. Some of them have video footage of people telling stories about California history. There's even a game you can play that takes you around the gallery to try to find certain objects. It's a way to have a little fun and learn more about the state's history at the same time.

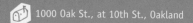 1000 Oak St., at 10th St., Oakland

510/238-2200 or 888/625-6873, 510/238-3818 Family Explorations!

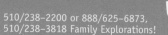 $6 adults, $4 children 6–17 and students

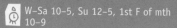 W–Sa 10–5, Su 12–5, 1st F of mth 10–9

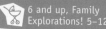 6 and up, Family Explorations! 5–12

Art, you'll find some 500 paintings, sculptures, prints, photographs, and decorative arts produced by California artists from the early 19th century to the present. Watch for sketches and paintings by early artist-explorers, Gold Rush genre pictures, colorful landscapes, and more modern Bay Area Pop and Funk works.

The museum hosts major temporary exhibitions in its Great Hall—covering such varied topics as hot-rod culture, California caves and subterranean habitats, and objects made with recycled materials—and the museum's courtyards often are the site of open-air art exhibitions. In addition, Family Explorations! programs allow parents and kids to experience the museum together, watch performances, and make artworks to take home.

**KID-FRIENDLY EATS** The museum's **OMCA Café** features hot entrées, sandwiches, soups, salads, snacks, and desserts. Another option is to spread out a blanket under the shade trees along the banks of Lake Merritt and have a picnic. Nearby **Zza's Trattoria** (*see* Children's Fairyland) is a child-friendly Italian restaurant.

# OAKLAND ZOO

The Oakland Zoo is a case study in how much some zoos have progressed of late. Once known as one of the worst zoos in the country, with cramped and depressing animal enclosures, it embarked on a long-term renovation program in the 1980s and now has facilities approaching those in some of the state's top zoos. It comprises 50 different exhibits on 100 acres within Knowland Park, harboring more than 300 native and exotic animals.

Just inside the entrance, you're greeted by bright pink flamingos in Flamingo Plaza, which makes a good orientation or meeting point. Head off to the right for the African Veldt area, where giraffes, gazelles, lions, and elephants reside. You can get a bird's-eye view of the African veldt—as well as bison, elk, and other animals—from the Skyride, but this 15-minute ride might scare young kids, since the open cars go quite high.

Straight ahead of Flamingo Plaza are the monkey, ape, and chimp habitats, perhaps the zoo's most interesting area. On especially lush, tropical Siamang Island and Gibbon Island, hooting

**KEEP IN MIND** Kids aged 4–12, as well as teens up to 17, are eligible for the popular summertime Zoo Camp, a series of one-week sessions during July and August that introduce kids to the zoo's wildlife. Each week has a theme, such as "fur, feathers, scales, and skin," but these change each year. Depending on ages and whether or not you choose a half-day or full-day program, fees range from $65 to $175 per week. Each child is limited to one week. Call the zoo's education department several months in advance for reservations.

9777 Golf Links Rd., Knowland Park, Oakland

 Daily 10–4, weather permitting

 510/632-9525

$6.50 ages 15 and up, $3.50
children 2–14; Skyride $1.50

 All ages

primates swing through the trees in a rain-forest environment. One of the zoo's newest exhibits, the African Savanna, simulates desert areas of eastern and southern Africa. It's landscaped with man-made rocks, a waterfall, and Kikuyu-style "mud and cow dung" (actually disguised concrete) structures; the 20 species who call it home include warthogs, hyenas, green monkeys, and meerkats. Your children will probably enjoy climbing into a tube for a "meerkat's-eye view" of the savanna.

And don't miss the Children's Zoo (free with admission). Here your kids can watch river otters, bobcats, pythons, iguanas, and alligators and can pet and feed domestic sheep and pygmy goats. It really brings the zoo experience up close and personal.

**KID-FRIENDLY EATS** Besides the zoo's standard food concessions, Knowland Park has plenty of grassy picnic areas with tables and barbecue facilities. For restaurants in Oakland's family-friendly Lake Merritt area (take I–580 west from the zoo to the Grand Avenue exit), *see* Children's Fairyland.

**HEY, KIDS!** You can ride around part of the zoo on a miniature train called the *C.P. Huntington*, a ⅔- size replica of a Civil War–era locomotive. The cost is $1.50 per ride. Look for the carousel, too, as well as some small carnival-type rides, but be sure to check the height limits to make sure you're not too big!

# OCEAN BEACH

San Francisco's best-known beach is a wide, mostly flat, 4-mile blanket of sand that forms the western, Pacific Ocean edge of the city, across the Great Highway from Golden Gate Park. It stretches south from the Cliff House to Ft. Funston (*see above*), which occupy cliffs overlooking the beach from opposite directions.

On warm, sunny days, the beach is typically packed with sunbathers, Frisbee tossers, dog walkers, and kite-flyers taking advantage of the ocean breezes—and sometimes gusty winds. This is also a favored spot for watching the sunset. Some people never get out of their parked cars! Even on foggy, misty days—and there are many here—Ocean Beach is a gathering place for a diverse group of people in search of recreation. Anglers cast their lines for perch and stripers. Just below the Cliff House, expert surfers ride the waves. (This is not a place for beginners.) Because of the often rough, treacherous surf, swimming is one activity that's not recommended; currents are unpredictable, undertow is strong, and there are no lifeguards. Besides, the water is just plain cold, suitable mainly for polar bears.

**KID-FRIENDLY EATS** For restaurants in and near the Cliff House, *see* the Cliff House. Another option is the **Beach Chalet** (*see* Golden Gate Park), across the Great Highway from Ocean Beach. Otherwise, just bring your own food and have a picnic on the beach.

**HEY, KIDS!** If you hear barking, it may not be a dog, but a sea lion. Sea lions like to soak up the sunshine on Seal Rocks, at the far northern end of Ocean Beach, just below the Cliff House. Despite the name Seal Rocks, harbor seals only come here occasionally—not nearly as much as the sea lions do—and they don't bark. Even though seals and sea lions look a lot alike, they aren't closely related.

One of the main draws of Ocean Beach runs right alongside it for the first mile or so down from the Cliff House: a broad paved pathway that attracts cyclists, Rollerbladers, joggers, walkers, and parents pushing strollers. Another pathway runs along the opposite side of the Great Highway, bordering Golden Gate Park, and remains paved all the way to Sloat Boulevard, about 3 miles away, where you can connect with the bike path around Lake Merced (*see above*). Because you'll ride on the road a bit toward the end, the latter portion of the bike route is suitable for older kids only.

Yet despite all the activity, Ocean Beach remains essentially unspoiled and free of commercial development. No buildings block ocean views; no concessions operate south of the Cliff House. It's a place where both local and visiting families can find fun, in sun or fog.

*KEEP IN MIND* Here are a few things to remember when visiting Ocean Beach. In summer, the beach is often foggy, windy, and chilly, and sweatshirts may be more appropriate than swimsuits. (San Francisco's warmest months are typically May and September.) If your children are brave enough to stick their toes in the water, be especially careful about keeping an eye on them. A sneaker wave could come along and easily pull a wading child out to sea. Remember, there are no lifeguards.

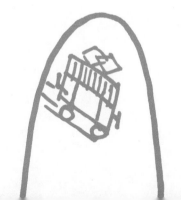

# PARAMOUNT'S GREAT AMERICA

Tackling the roller coasters and other daredevil rides at this movie- and TV-theme park is nothing less than a rite of passage for many Bay Area youngsters. Ten-year-olds who board the Vortex for a heart-thumping stand-up roller coaster ride know they're growing up; 12-year-olds who brave a 22-story, 91-feet-per-second open-air fall on the Drop Zone can claim bragging rights all winter over those who held back.

Top Gun, a jet coaster meant to simulate the sensations of flying an F-14 Tomcat jet fighter, provides short but intense thrills. As you catapult off into space at 50 mph, you experience a 360° vertical loop, two 270° "afterburn turns," and a "zero-gravity barrel roll." One of the stomach-turners here, Invertigo, was the first suspended, inverted face-to-face coaster in North America; it takes riders forward and backward at 55 mph through a boomerang and vertical loop. And James Bond 007: A License to Thrill is a motion simulator ride that takes would-be Bonds on motorcycle and jet-ski chases as well as skydiving from a helicopter.

**KEEP IN MIND** Here are some tips to get the most out of your day. Note that most of the scarier rides have minimum height requirements and that some of the kiddie rides have maximum height requirements (adults have to be accompanied by kids). Explaining this to children of borderline height might ward off disappointment. If your kids plan to visit Splat City or go on the water rides, bring a change of clothing, or have them wear swimsuits. For your own and your littlest one's comfort, use the park's baby-care center (a changing, feeding, and nursing facility) and stroller rentals, as necessary.

Younger kids aren't forgotten. At Nickelodeon Splat City, a 3-acre tribute to messiness, everyone is guaranteed to get drenched with gallons of water and Green Slime. The classic double-deck Carousel Columbia, near the park's front entrance, is the world's tallest. Great America also has mid-range rides that are exciting but less scary than Top Gun or Invertigo for squeamish (or should we say careful?) youngsters or parents. Among these are the Grizzly, a classic wooden roller coaster, and three water rides, including Rip Roaring Rapids, a rafting ride that's great for getting soaked on a hot day.

For a quieter way to cool off and wind down, the park offers a number of stage shows containing music, cartoon characters, and, in some cases, audience participation. There's also a seven-story IMAX theater. In all, there's plenty to entertain every member of the family—whether fearless or prudent.

**KID-FRIENDLY EATS** Among park concessions, **Shaggy's Snack Shack,** in Kidzville, has burgers and fries, as does the **American Grill,** a '50s-style diner in Orleans Place. **Wings,** in Yukon Territory, carries rotisserie chicken and chili. The **Pasta Connection** is in Yankee Harbor, and **Maggie Brown's,** in Hometown Square, has chicken dinners.

**HEY, KIDS!** Kidzville, added to Great America in 1999 (you'll find it right next to Splat City), was built for young kids. It has 18 rides, including the Taxi Jam mini-roller coaster and the Junior Jump Club, where you can dare your parents to join you on a parachute drop. It doesn't go *too* high, so Mom and Dad shouldn't get too scared. There's also a play-crawl space called the Kidz Construction Company, plus entertainment by cartoon characters like Fred Flintstone and Yogi Bear.

# PIER 39

This once-abandoned, decaying, 1,000-foot cargo pier on the eastern edge of Fisherman's Wharf (*see above*) was transformed into a waterside shopping mall in the late 1970s, and it's been San Francisco's top tourist draw ever since. Publicists claim it's the third-most-popular attraction in the United States after Walt Disney World and Disneyland.

Although many San Franciscans consider it a tacky tourist trap, local kids still head here in droves, alongside the out-of-towners. It's a lot like going to a seaside carnival. It costs nothing to walk in or drink up the wonderful bay views. For those, just follow the wooden boardwalks to the sides or rear of the pier. Rest assured, however: There are plenty of places to lighten your wallet. More than 100 shops, 10 restaurants, and several fast-food stands line the double-deck pier, including places to buy toys and candy.

Entertainment abounds. An antique double-deck Venetian carousel entices younger children. Turbo Ride, a motion-simulated adventure ride, is popular with preteens and teens, who

## KID-FRIENDLY EATS
Pier 39 is loaded with snack shops. The specialties at the **Boudin Sourdough Bakery & Café** (tel. 415/421–0185) are clam chowder and chili in a bread bowl, great on a cool, foggy day. For other restaurants on the Pier, *see* Alcatraz Island.

**HEY, KIDS!** There are two large arcades at Pier 39 (tel. 415/399–9907 for both), filled with video games and other games of skill, like air hockey and ice ball, plus bumper cars. Namco Land is geared toward younger kids, while Cyberstation is for ages 12 and up. If you do well at the Cyberstation games, you win tickets that you can exchange for small prizes, like toys and candy.

The Embarcadero, at Jefferson and Powell Sts.

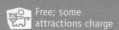 415/981-7437, 415/956-3456
movie theater

 Free; some
attractions charge

 Daily 10-10

3 and up

also flock to arcades to test themselves at video games and bumper cars. The Citibank Cinemax Theatre shows *The Great San Francisco Adventure* and other films. The UnderWater World aquarium (*see below*) sits off to one side. The pier also houses the Blue & Gold Fleet of sightseeing ferries (*see* Bay Cruises) along with a large marina.

Those with iron willpower or slender budgets, however, can spend enjoyable hours here with little cash outlay. Jugglers, yo-yo artists, magicians, clowns, and other entertainers perform for loose change. But the best show may be a colony of California sea lions, which took up residence at the West Marina here in 1990 and have been delighting onlookers ever since. Their numbers vary greatly depending on the time of year (winter is best, summer slimmest), but it's not unusual for several hundred of the playful, often smelly, thousand-pound pinnipeds to provide captivating displays of barking, frolicking, and jockeying for sunbathing position on the docks—and they don't even pass the hat at the end.

KEEP IN MIND Naturally, the sea lions don't have open and closed hours, and you can watch them here any day of the week. However, to learn more about them, try to come for one of the free guided talks, offered on weekends 12–4 by docents from Marin County's Marine Mammal Center (*see* Marin Headlands).

# PRESIDIO NATIONAL PARK

Until recently, this nearly 1,500-acre park overlooking the Golden Gate was a military post, as it had been for more than two centuries. The Spanish came in 1776, establishing a walled fortification (or *presidio*) to protect the bay and Mission Dolores (*see above*). After passing into Mexico's hands in 1822, the Presidio fell to the United States when it acquired California in 1846; it became the Sixth Army's base and a training ground for Civil War soldiers. In 1994, the Army moved out, and the Presidio became part of the Golden Gate National Recreation Area. Plans for the park are still being developed, and full conversion to recreational and other uses will take time. (Some commercial-related developments, such as a mostly private film "campus" being built by *Star Wars* creator George Lucas, have proven controversial.) But already the Presidio contains miles of bike routes and hiking trails that wind along coastal bluffs, past hundreds of historic military buildings and defense installations, and over hills thick with cypress, eucalyptus, and pine trees. At many points, hikers and cyclists get dazzling views of the bay, the Golden Gate Bridge, and the Marin Headlands.

**HEY, KIDS!** Visit the Presidio Pet Cemetery, where military families buried their furry loved ones, and pause to appreciate the pictures, poems, and sweet epitaphs their owners attached to their gravestones. The cemetery is located off Lincoln Boulevard near the old stables, almost right under the bridge approach and not far from the National Cemetery, where soldiers are buried. It's a little hard to find: Look for the white picket fence; if you have trouble, ask for directions at the visitor center.

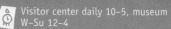
 Main gate, Lombard and Lyon Sts.; visitor center, Lincoln Blvd. and Montgomery St.

 Free

 Visitor center daily 10–5, museum W–Su 12–4

415/561–4323 visitor center, 415/556–0560 park service

All ages

In addition to learning some Presidio history at Fort Point National Historic Site (*see above*), you can soak some up at the Presidio Army Museum, which contains uniforms, maps, weapons, and displays on the 1906 San Francisco earthquake and the 1915 Panama-Pacific Exposition. Outside are a pair of green cottages that homeless survivors of the 1906 quake rented for $2 a month.

At Crissy Field, which includes a beach on the Presidio's bay side, you can picnic, bike, skate, fly kites, or go windsurfing (it's too rough for beginners, though). Brave souls swim at Baker Beach, a scenic stretch of sand west of the Golden Gate Bridge, but the surf is dangerous. The Presidio Golf Course and nearby Julius Kahn playground—with basketball and tennis courts, a softball field, and plentiful grass for picnics—are in the park's southern reaches. The Presidio Bowling Center completes an array of onetime military recreational facilities now open to the public.

**KID-FRIENDLY EATS** The Presidio has several good picnic areas, and there are barbecue facilities behind Baker Beach and other locations. For information about the Presidio's **Burger King** with a view, *see* Fort Point National Historic Site. For restaurants near the Presidio, *see* the California Palace of the Legion of Honor and the Exploratorium.

**KEEP IN MIND** The Presidio Visitors Information Center has maps, brochures, trail guides, and schedules for guided walks and bike tours. On weekends, free ranger-led walks last from 45 minutes to three hours and cover the Presidio's natural history, the area's strategic military history, and the bay-side tidal zone. They're best for ages 10 and up.

# RANDALL MUSEUM

This small children's museum is so far off the beaten path that it's a wonder anyone ever finds it. Yet among San Francisco parents-in-the-know, it's considered a treasure whose value far outweighs its size. Overlooking the city in Corona Heights Park, the Randall occupies a dramatic perch above Buena Vista Park, between the Haight-Ashbury and Castro districts. Inside, the museum is chock-full of intriguing hands-on exhibits in the realms of nature, art, and science.

Your children will find minerals to touch, dinosaur bones to peruse, and chemistry and biology labs to test out. An earthquake exhibit has a working seismograph, a model of a refugee shack typical of those that housed homeless survivors of the 1906 San Francisco quake, a demonstration of how the earth's shifting tectonic plates can cause quakes, and a fun area called Make-a-Quake, in which kids get to jump up and down and see how much "seismic force" they can produce themselves. Probably the museum's most popular feature, though, is its live animal room, where your children can learn about and get close-up looks at

## HEY, KIDS!
Every spring, the Randall has a crafts fair and a festival where you can see clowns, hear bagpipes, and try cool games. On Halloween night, the Randall becomes a haunted house where you can play games, listen to scary stories, carve pumpkins, and look at animals whose eyes glow in the dark.

**KEEP IN MIND** Corona Heights Park offers one of the great "hidden" overlooks of San Francisco. The views are a real bonus, especially for parents, but older kids often enjoy the steep climb to the top. The treasure for young kids is a playground with swings and sand, and there are tennis and basketball courts, too. For the latter three activities, follow paths down the hill from the museum.

199 Museum Way (off Roosevelt Way)

 T–Sa 10–5, animal talks Sa 11

415/554–9600

Donations accepted; some programs charge

3 and up, field trips 8 and up

critters such as owls, snakes, mice, and raccoons. Young kids especially take to the petting corral, where they can stroke rabbits and ducks. Staff members give free Saturday animal talks.

The museum has put together a strong program for families. Year-round, the Randall offers nature and art classes (registration required) that last 8 to 10 weeks for one hour per week. Art classes might include woodworking, ceramics, and jewelry-making; nature classes might focus on biology or the environment. Teenagers can attend the Cine/Club, where they can watch and critique films. The Randall also has drop-in workshops, given twice on Saturdays, that feature a variety of hands-on activities, and sponsors scheduled field trips, such as hikes to see migrating geese. Call the museum or stop by for current schedules and prices.

*KID-FRIENDLY EATS* At **Sweet Heat** (1725 Haight St., tel. 415/387–8845), you can pick up inexpensive tacos and burritos to take up to Corona Heights Park, or, if you've already visited the Randall, to nearby Golden Gate Park. A few blocks east down the hill from the museum is **Sparky's Diner** (242 Church St., tel. 415/621–6001), where you can get diner-style breakfasts or burgers and fries.

# SAN FRANCISCO BAY NATIONAL
## WILDLIFE REFUGE

Lying just north of San Jose on the southern reaches of San Francisco Bay, this was the country's first urban wildlife refuge, founded in 1972, and it's still one of the most popular—both with wildlife and humans. With 43,000 protected acres along 25 miles of shoreline, the refuge has an extensive system of boardwalks and trails for hiking and cycling, from which you can view wildlife in the salt ponds, marshes, and mudflats. During fall and spring migrations, it's a way station for more than a million shorebirds, waterfowl, and wading birds: sandpipers, peregrine falcons, snowy egrets, great blue herons, canvasback ducks, mallards, kites, terns, and brown pelicans. Harbor seals also often hang around.

Administered by the U.S. Fish and Wildlife Service, the refuge is part of a large complex of U.S.-run refuges in the Bay Area, including the Farallon National Wildlife Refuge (*see above*). Stop at the visitor center to see exhibits, use the observation deck, and pick up trail information. Several trailheads are nearby. A dozen more miles of trails, as well as more displays and an observation deck, are found several miles away at the refuge's Environmental

**HEY, KIDS!** Be sure to bring a pair of binoculars to search for birds, lizards, snakes, and rabbits. Also, ask the refuge staff about borrowing a free wildlife or environmental video; some choices include *Who Did the Owl Eat?*, *Secrets of the Bay*, *Into the Wild*, and *It's Wet, It's Wild, It's Water!* You won't find those at Blockbuster Video.

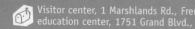

Education Center, near the town of Alviso; call for directions, which are complicated, or pick up a map at the visitor center. Another, less used portion of the refuge (with one trail) is located across the Dumbarton Bridge near the town of Redwood City, on the western side of San Francisco Bay.

The refuge celebrates National Wildlife Refuge Week each October with a variety of programs of interest to families, including campfire sing-alongs and puppet shows, twilight hikes, bicycling, and environmental education programs (such as Shark Day, when guided walks teach about local sharks and you can make yourself a shark T-shirt). The refuge also has an annual daytime Halloween Party. But the real treat is what you'll see here any day of the year.

**KID-FRIENDLY EATS** There are picnic facilities near the visitor center as well as a couple of picnic tables adjacent to the education center, but remember that the refuge is not a park—you must pack out your trash. The nearest restaurants to the visitor center are a collection of fast-food places about 2 miles away on Jarvis Avenue in Newark *(see* Ardenwood Historic Farm).

**KEEP IN MIND** Pick up an activities schedule listing weekend family hikes, and then lace up your hiking boots. On these two-hour outings, you can discover the habitat of the salt-marsh harvest mouse—an endangered species—and see rabbits, snakes, lizards, birds, and other wildlife. Slow and easy bike tours are offered, too, but you and your kids should each have a mountain bike and, of course, be old enough (or young enough) to ride one.

# SAN FRANCISCO MAIN LIBRARY

This library, which opened in 1996, can be quite an entertaining place, starting with the talking elevators. As you ride, a voice calls out helpful information like "going up," "please turn right," and "first floor." But then libraries are full of helpful information, and this is one of the most technologically advanced in the country. It has some 300 computer terminals, many with free Internet access and CD-ROM capability; sizable video and music collections; and, of course, a good many books. You can enjoy all this in an architecturally striking, modern building that's airy and light and has plenty of open space.

Head to the Fisher Children's Center, on the second floor, where librarians expect kids to be noisy and the atmosphere is exciting, not stuffy. Here you'll find the Electronic Discovery Center, loaded with computers where your children can read stories or play video games. If you're concerned they'll do too much of the latter at the expense of the former, you may accompany them to explore what's available. Each child is allowed one 30-minute session per day, and then can opt to go on a waiting list for another 30 minutes.

**KEEP IN MIND** Across the street in the Civic Center Plaza, there's a playground for elementary schoolkids, with tire swings, slides, and monkey bars. It's a good stop after your little one has been quiet and still in the library for too long. City Hall, with its gleaming copper dome, is across the plaza.

**HEY, KIDS!** The library offers all kinds of programs for kids. You can watch a magician or a movie or learn hip-hop dancing, Japanese drumming, or Mexican paper cutting. There are also celebrations and festivals centered on different cultures, so ask your parents to pick up a monthly schedule. All classes are free, and you don't even have to live in San Francisco.

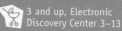
Connected to the Electronic Discovery Center is a big children's reading room and story room, with lots of desks and corners to sit in. (On Saturday mornings, there are story times for families of preschoolers, which last about ½ hour.) In another room, your kids can watch scheduled movies and participate in programs where they can learn crafts or be otherwise entertained. Teenagers should check out the third-floor Teen Center, where books are geared to their age group. Elsewhere, you'll find collections of San Francisco memorabilia, an African-American Center, an Asian-American Center, and special art and photo exhibitions. A roof garden and terrace on the sixth floor is for all to use. If you want your family to get a sense of what's where, take one of the thrice-weekly tours, most suitable for fourth graders and up.

**KID-FRIENDLY EATS** The small but pleasant **Library Café** (tel. 415/437–4838), on the lower level, has sandwiches, salads, and soups at reasonable prices. **Max's Opera Café** (601 Van Ness Ave., tel. 415/771–7300) serves sandwiches and other meals with portions big enough for a small family to share; don't be surprised if your server, who may be an aspiring opera singer, breaks into song in the evening.

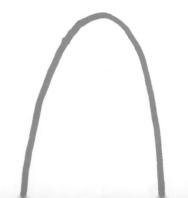

# SAN FRANCISCO MARITIME
## NATIONAL HISTORIC PARK

The Hyde Street Pier, part of the San Francisco Maritime National Historic Park, is the site of the world's largest fleet of historic ships (by tonnage) and the country's only floating national park. This is a great spot to introduce kids to what shipboard life was like in the days before *The Love Boat*.

The *Balclutha*, an 1886 steel-hulled, square-rigged sailing ship, is the flagship vessel. The 300-foot-long windjammer was launched in Scotland and navigated Cape Horn 17 times before ending its days transporting Alaskan salmon from the Bering Sea to San Francisco (when it was known as the *Star of Alaska*). Most kids enjoy clambering down its narrow ladders and around its claustrophobic decks for looks at its restored cabins.

Several other ships are also on display. The *C.A. Thayer* is a three-masted schooner built in 1895 to move the lumber that helped build many early California cities. San Francisco Bay's oldest ferry, the paddle-wheeler *Eureka,* dates from 1890 and was once the world's largest

**KEEP IN MIND** Aquatic Park (tel. 415/556–1238), just below the National Maritime Museum at the foot of Polk Street, is a good place to relax after touring the ships or museum. Kids can wade in the gentle (though cold) water at a sandy beach, and you can lay out a blanket and sunbathe or picnic on the manicured lawns. Every fall, you can watch a sand castle–building contest (tel. 415/512–1899) on the beach, in which local schoolkids compete with local architects. A short walk away, the Municipal Pier provides a favorite fishing spot and great bay views.

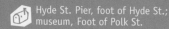
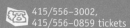
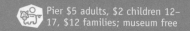
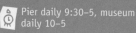

auto and passenger ferry. The 1891 scow schooner *Alma* has a flat bottom that enabled her to navigate the shallow waters on the periphery of the bay, where she hauled hay. And the *Hercules* was a steam-powered ocean tug that is boardable at high tide only. Special family events—sail-raisings, sea chantey songfests, evening concerts—are held here periodically.

The National Maritime Museum, housed in a 1930s Art Deco building, is also part of the national historic park. Highlights include a collection of intricately crafted ship models along with rows of carved figureheads that once adorned the bows of Gold Rush–era clippers. Photos, maps, diaries, and ships' logs also help chronicle West Coast maritime history.

**KID-FRIENDLY EATS** Aquatic Park is a nice place to picnic, and there are also snack bars here. For restaurants in this area, *see* Fisherman's Wharf and the Cannery and Ghirardelli Square.

**HEY, KIDS!** Imagine the scene before the Golden Gate and Bay bridges enabled people to drive across the bay. In the early 20th century, thousands of passengers boarded the *Eureka* every day to ride to Marin County, Oakland, or Berkeley. The *Eureka* also served as "the tracks across the bay," as it carried train travelers from around the country on the final leg of their journey: from Oakland to San Francisco. As long as you're imagining, just imagine their relief!

# SAN FRANCISCO MUSEUM OF MODERN ART

It's true that few kids (and few parents, for that matter) can tell abstract expressionism from analytical cubism, or Surrealism from op art. And as for Dada, he's with Mama. But children are often drawn to the typically bright colors and geometric shapes of modern and contemporary art. The San Francisco Museum of Modern Art—or SF-MOMA for somewhat short—is now the country's second-largest modern art museum.

Across from the Yerba Buena Center for the Arts, the bright, airy six-story museum, which opened in 1995, is topped by a 145-foot-tall skylight tower. In fact, the building itself is one of the main attractions. The permanent collections—15,000 pieces, only a small portion of which is displayed at one time—highlight painting and sculpture from 1900 to 1970. Picasso, Braque, Klee, Dalí, Matisse, Diebenkorn, Pollock, de Kooning, Rivera, and Kahlo are all here. Architecture and design, 20th-century photography (by Man Ray and Ansel Adams, among others), and special exhibits are also featured, along with video, audio, and interactive media installations—ranging from "weird" to "awesome" in the words of some young visitors.

## KEEP IN MIND

As the museum admits, some artworks have "challenging content or explicit imagery" and may not be appropriate for children. If this is a concern for you, preview the museum yourself before visiting with kids. That way, you'll know which rooms (if any) to avoid.

**HEY, KIDS!** Tell Mom and Dad about the museum's twice-yearly Family Days, when each adult who comes with a child pays just $2 (kids, including high school students, are free). On those days, one in June and one in October from 11 to 4, you can do hands-on art projects, listen to music, watch performances, and take special tours of some of the galleries, too. Parents can find out more by calling the museum.

151 3rd St.

 $9 adults, $5 students 13 and up; Th 6–9 half-price; 1st T of mth free

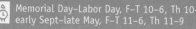 Memorial Day–Labor Day, F–T 10–6, Th 10–9; early Sept–late May, F–T 11–6, Th 11–9

415/357–4000, 415/357–4097 family programs, 415/357–4035 store

 3 and up

The MuseumStore is superb. Art books, art supplies, prints, posters, and jewelry are for sale, and there's a wonderful section of children's art books and educational toys. Kids can even try out some toys on the spot. The ground-level store is open daily, and you can shop without paying museum admission.

SF-MOMA is committed to drawing kids and families into the world of modern art. On Family Sundays, families can drop in to the Koret Education Center (12–3) for a free hands-on art studio directed by guest artists. The workshop may include drawing, painting, collage, printmaking, or assemblage. On some spring and summer Saturdays, parents and young children can together explore color and form in a program called Children's Art Studio. The seven one-hour sessions are for ages 2½–4 (11–12) and ages 4–6 (12:30–1:30), also at the Koret Education Center. After all, what's seeing without doing?

## KID-FRIENDLY EATS **Caffe Museo** (tel. 415/357–4500),

on the ground floor of the museum, serves soups, focaccia sandwiches, and morning pastries; it's open during museum hours, including Thursday evenings. Across the street, a branch of **Pasqua Coffee** (*see* Yerba Buena Gardens) has fresh-made panini (Italian-style) sandwiches (roast turkey pesto, roast beef Parmesan, fresh mozzarella), salads, baked goods, coffees, and hot cocoa. Outdoor tables offer nice views.

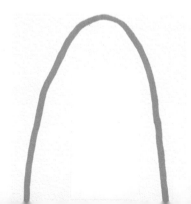

# SAN FRANCISCO ZOO

Set on 125 acres in the fog belt way out toward the ocean, this is Northern California's largest zoo. More than 1,000 birds and animals representing 220 species reside here, and several facilities now rank with the best in the state.

You might want to start at the 7-acre Children's Zoo, located right near the front entrance. Your kids can pet farm animals in the Barnyard and peer at creepy-crawlies in the big indoor Insect Zoo. The Children's Zoo also has a baby-animal nursery, a deer park, a nature trail, a nature theater, and a chick hatchery.

Elsewhere, at the Primate Discovery Center, colobus and patas monkeys, white ruffed lemurs, and macaques live and play in a spectacular bilevel setting; don't miss the interactive learning exhibits on the ground level. In the Kresge Nocturnal Gallery, next door, careful searching will yield views (however dim) of lemurs and other night creatures; children who are afraid of the dark may find this a bit spooky. A fair walk away, a three-generation family of lowland

**KEEP IN MIND** The big cats are fed Tuesday–Sunday at 2; penguins are fed daily at 3. Both are entertaining, as are Meet the Keeper talks, given by zookeepers; check for a schedule. The Wildlife Theater stages shows late June–Labor Day, Tuesday–Sunday. This is one good place to rest if you're tired of walking. Another is the narrated Safari Train that circles the zoo ($2.50 ages 6 and up, $1.50 children 5 and under). If you're happy walking but your child isn't, stroller rentals are available. And remember that the zoo is a CityPass attraction (*see* the California Academy of Sciences).

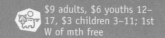

gorillas lives in spacious Gorilla World—one of the most luxurious such exhibits in the world. On Penguin Island, dozens of Magellanic penguins dive into a 200-foot pool. In the Australian Walkabout, kangaroos and wallabies hop about, while in Koala Crossing, koalas cling shyly to the trees.

Fifty rainbow lorikeets occupy a walk-through aviary in the new Rainbow Landing. The *Puente al Sur* ("Bridge to the South") exhibit contains 7 acres of rain forest, where tapirs, Andean condors, and howler monkeys roam. The zoo is also home to rare and endangered species, such as the black rhino, orangutan, Madagascar aye-aye, and, in the Feline Conservation Center, cats such as the ocelet and jaguar. The usual complements of elephants, warthogs, giraffes, and lions and tigers and bears are on hand as well. Oh my!

**KID-FRIENDLY EATS** The zoo contains the usual hot dog and ice cream concession stands. After you're done at the zoo, head across the street to **Leon's Bar-B-Q** (*see* Ft. Funston) or a bit farther to **Just Won Ton** (1241 Vicente St., tel. 415/681–2999), where you can get warming bowls of Chinese wonton soup or noodle dishes; it's small, informal, and inexpensive.

**HEY, KIDS!** During the Livestock Stampede in the Barnyard at the Children's Zoo, you can help feed breakfast to the goats and sheep. Be there at 10:45 in summer, 11:15 on fall weekends. You can also ride the carousel or the Little Puffer miniature steam train, each of which costs $2 (as does the Children's Zoo on free Wednesdays), and check out the playground near the Children's Zoo.

# SIX FLAGS MARINE WORLD

Formerly Marine World Africa USA, Six Flags Marine World is an ambitious combination of wildlife park, oceanarium, and amusement park, all packed into 160 acres about 35 miles northeast of San Francisco. If your children want to feed a giraffe, ride an elephant, watch a water-ski show, or ride a roller coaster, they can do it here. Though amusement-park rides, all opened since 1998, are becoming a big part of the scene, the park's traditional mainstays are its nine shows.

The Dolphin Harbor stadium provides a slick showcase for bottle-nosed dolphins, who jump 20 feet out of the water and do tail walks, flips, air spins, and other "behaviors" (in the old days, we called them "tricks"). Acrylic panels allow your kids to watch the dolphins underwater, too. Killer whales, all 6,000 pounds of them, jump, swim, and dive in rhythm in their own stadium. The Tiger Island Splash Attack provides an underwater view of a dozen Bengal tigers at play. In other shows, sea lions do high dives, elephants demonstrate their agility, birds swoop and squawk, and daring two-legged mammals perform stunts on water skis and

## HEY, KIDS!

If you sit up front at the killer whale show, you'll get soaked, and you might be chosen to get kissed by one. At other shows, kids are also picked to touch the animals. If you aren't, look for trainers, who often walk around with camels, llamas, or reindeer and may let you touch one.

**KEEP IN MIND** Pick up a daily schedule, and plan your itinerary as soon as you enter the park to make sure you cover as many shows, rides, and attractions as you can fit in. The 20- to 25-minute shows are offered at various times throughout the day, and, on busy days, good seats go early. If you can get to the park by the time it opens or shortly after, you'll have fewer crowds to fight, starting with the parking lot and entrance lines.

do 32-foot free falls. In all but the latter two shows, trainers lace the entertainment with lessons on how animals survive—and are endangered—in the wild.

Among other animal-related exhibits, Shark Experience has a moving ramp through a clear tunnel in a huge shark tank, while Walkabout! An Australian Adventure and the separate Walrus Experience provide close-up views of kangaroos, wallaroos, wallabies, koalas, and walruses. At Giraffe Dock, your kids can hand-feed the giraffes; at Elephant Encounter, they can ride or play tug-of-war with an elephant (both of these cost extra).

Scattered throughout the park, assorted non-animal rides range from a 150-foot-tall, three-loop roller coaster (which travels forwards and backwards at 50 mph), spinning teacups, and a Ferris wheel to a river-rapids ride, a train, paddleboats, and a dinosaur-theme 3-D motion-simulator ride. Looney Tunes Seaport is a fun zone with rides geared to kids 10 and under, including a carousel and a submarine.

**KID-FRIENDLY EATS** Concessions at the park include **Pizza Safari** (for pizza) and the **Broiler** (for burgers and fries), both of which have outdoor tables. **Sports Bottle Crepe** has both sweet and savory crepes and is a step up from standard theme-park food. **Mobe's** has fish and chicken sandwiches, and for dessert, the **Pink Flamingo** is the spot for flavored ices and cotton candy.

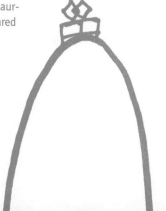

# STERN GROVE FESTIVAL

Every parent knows that taking young kids to an indoor concert can be a kicking, squirming disaster. This festival offers a chance to introduce children to a variety of musical styles—even opera and symphony—without the worry or the cost. Sigmund Stern Grove—a 63-acre stand of eucalyptus, redwood, and fir trees in the Sunset District—provides a shady setting and natural amphitheater for the nation's oldest free outdoor concert series; it's been running each summer since 1937.

The grove, a gift to the city from the widow of a local civic and business leader, extends down steep hillsides to a valley, where a grassy meadow looks up to a stage. Some seating is available directly in front of the stage; the most select includes picnic tables available by reservation (also free) for a maximum party of six (call 415/831–5500 at 9 AM on the Monday preceding the concert). Most of the audience stretches out or sits on the grass or finds a perch on the tree-lined hillsides to the rear, which are decidedly less comfortable. The ideal approach is to bring a picnic lunch, arrive early (no later than 12, by midmorning for a good

**KEEP IN MIND** To pass the time while waiting for the concert, bring the Sunday paper, some toys or books for the kids, and plenty of snacks. While the trees usually offer some protection from winds, summertime is fog time near the coast, and Stern Grove often gets cool or even cold by midafternoon. Everyone should dress in layers, but don't forget the sunscreen, because it's often sunny between about 11 and 2.

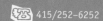

view), and spread a blanket or set low-slung lawn chairs out on the grass. Then sit back and enjoy the performance.

There are few more pleasant ways for a family to enjoy such a wide range of music and dance: Classical, opera, ballet, ethnic dance, jazz, rhythm and blues, gospel, and Latin music are all likely to take the stage over the course of the summer. While the schedule varies from year to year, you can usually expect appearances by the San Francisco Girls and Boys choruses, the San Francisco Symphony, San Francisco Opera, San Francisco Ballet, and the Preservation Hall Jazz Band. The latter has been coming to Stern Grove for more than 30 years and plays infectious, toe-tapping New Orleans–style jazz, usually the weekend nearest July 4. So let your toes loose, and tap away.

**HEY, KIDS:** There's a time for listening and watching and a time for playing. Sometimes you just have to play. For that, there's a small playground (partially hidden by trees) just inside the 19th Avenue entrance on the Sloat Boulevard side of Stern Grove.

**KID-FRIENDLY EATS** Several concession stands set up shop during the concerts. Look for burgers, knishes, and ice cream bars. After the performance, head to a nearby branch of **Chevys** (3251 20th Ave., Stonestown Shopping Center, tel. 415/665–8705), serving good Tex-Mex food with children's menus; kids can watch the tortilla-making machine. **Just Won Ton** (*see* the San Francisco Zoo) is good for informal, inexpensive Chinese food.

# TECH MUSEUM OF INNOVATION

**7**

oaded with custom-designed interactive exhibits, the Tech Museum is devoted solely to technology—in particular the innovations in microelectronics, communications, robotics, and biotechnology that have emerged here in Silicon Valley. While the description may be a mouthful, the museum does a great job in helping to demystify technology and make it fun for kids—and their parents. Leaving behind its previously cramped quarters, the Tech moved into a new 132,000-square-foot mango-and-azure-color domed facility in the heart of downtown San Jose in 1998. Nearly 250 cutting-edge exhibits are now arranged in four theme areas, and they're meant not just to inform and entertain, but to inspire museum visitors of all ages to be innovative themselves.

Activities go beyond "hands-on" to "minds-on," as museum staffers put it. In the Life Tech gallery, you and your kids can "drive" a simulated bobsled, use sound waves to "see" inside yourself, or enter images of a human body for an inside look. In the Innovation gallery, you can visit a "cleanroom" to see how microchips (the stuff of Silicon Valley) are made,

**KEEP IN MIND** The TechStore (tel. 408/795–6276) is stuffed with gadgets, gizmos, puzzles, and CD-ROMS. You'll find anti-gravity tops that float in space, kits for building 3-D creatures, and plenty more. Enter at the risk of doubling the cost of your trip.

**HEY, KIDS!** You've probably heard about Silicon Valley, where America's computer industry was born. It's been called the most inventive place on earth, and the Tech Museum is right in the heart of it. The museum was started in 1990 to provide an inside look at the technology developments that usually take place behind Silicon Valley's closed doors. And just as the computer industry has grown since 1990, so has the museum; it's in a new building several times the original's size.

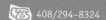

create your own futuristic bike design, and take an actual portrait of yourself with a laser scanner. In the Communication gallery, you and your kids can use teleconferencing equipment to communicate with one another on different floors of the museum. You can also experiment with the latest movie animation techniques—film yourself surfing, walking on the moon, or flying with Superman. And in the Exploration gallery, you can explore the ocean depths via an underwater, remote-controlled robot, test your ability to move around while weightless (as in a spaceship), and experience what it was like to shake through the 1906 and 1989 San Francisco earthquakes.

The museum also hosts traveling exhibits that showcase state-of-the-art, experimental technologies. The Hackworth IMAX Dome Theater has a hemispherical screen 82 feet in diameter and is the only one of its kind in Northern California. Call for tickets in advance (demand is high), and arrive 20 minutes prior to show time, as latecomers will not be seated.

**KID-FRIENDLY EATS** The museum's 80-seat **Café Primavera** (tel. 408/885–1094) has both indoor and outdoor seating. Sandwiches, salads, pizzas, and pastas are priced under $8, and there's a children's menu with burgers, hot dogs, sandwiches, and simple pastas. Just down the street at the landmark Fairmont Hotel, the **Fountain at the Fairmont** (170 S. Market St., tel. 408/998–1900) serves breakfast, lunch, and dinner in casual surroundings.

# TILDEN PARK

**6**

Tilden Park is the East Bay's answer to San Francisco's Golden Gate Park. With more than 2,000 acres, it's about twice the size of its better-known cousin across the bay, and its grassy lawns, rolling hills, and eucalyptus and pine groves are chock-full of recreation and picnic areas. Two lakes and peaks that rise to nearly 2,000 feet add form to the landscape. Woodsy hiking and biking trails lead throughout, and family attractions dot the park.

To the north, near the Cañon Drive entrance, is a pony ride concession, while in the central section, the 1911 antique Herschel-Spillman merry-go-round comes with hand-carved animals and a calliope. Both are open during school vacations and weekends. Nearby Lake Anza has a sandy beach, open May to October, that's popular for swimming. The water is generally sun-warmed and sheltered from the wind by hills, and lifeguards are on duty in season. You can also fish in the lake throughout the year. The botanic garden contains the world's most complete collection of California native plants.

**HEY, KIDS!** When you come to Tilden Park, be sure to visit the Little Farm (tel. 510/525–2233), where you can pet and feed sheep, rabbits, cows, pigs, and pygmy goats. The farm has a little barn and windmill, and there's a duck pond nearby. It's open 8:30–3:30 every day, and there's no charge.

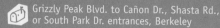 Grizzly Peak Blvd. to Cañon Dr., Shasta Rd., or South Park Dr. entrances, Berkeley

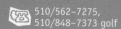 510/562-7275, 510/848-7373 golf

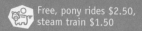 Free, pony rides $2.50, steam train $1.50

 Daily 5 AM–10 PM

 All ages

On the eastern edge of the park, the East Bay Skyline National Recreation Trail winds its way along the crest of the hills to Inspiration Point; the trail is accessible to hikers, horseback riders, and cyclists (the latter on fire road portions only) and links Tilden to other regional parks. Views stretch across the metropolitan Bay Area. In the far southeastern reaches of the park, the Tilden Park Steam Train, open during school vacations and weekends, lets families ride on a small steam train along a scenic ridge. Tilden also contains an 18-hole public golf course and driving range.

No matter what your children's (and your) ages and interests, you're sure to find something here to enjoy.

**KID-FRIENDLY EATS** There are numerous picnic areas, as well as concession stands at Lake Anza, the merry-go-round, and other park locations. For restaurants in Berkeley, *see* the Lawrence Hall of Science.

**KEEP IN MIND** The park's Environmental Education Center (tel. 510/525-2233), near the Little Farm, offers hiking, nature, and other programs for kids and families year-round. You can study the life of a pond or even learn how to make sushi. Some programs require reservations, and some require fees (usually $5–$25), so call to find out.

# UNDERWATER WORLD AT PIER 39

UnderWater World bills itself as America's first "diver's-eye view" aquarium, though others have opened since. Here you and your children walk in clear acrylic tunnels to view an array of sharks, bat rays, eels, sturgeon, sea stars, smelt, perch, and other creatures that dwell in San Francisco Bay. The concept is an intriguing one: People are, in effect, on the inside looking out into the tanks, while the marine life—swimming freely above and around the humans—are on the outside looking in.

At the beginning, there are some minor exhibits, but to reach the real draw, you have to descend in an elevator. Two 400-foot-long transparent tunnels take you "into" a two-story tank that holds more than 700,000 gallons of water and 10,000 creatures, so there's a lot to see. When you spot a shark swimming directly over your head—well, that's an experience not easily forgotten.

**KID-FRIENDLY EATS** If Under-Water World gets you hungry for seafood, with an emphasis on shrimp, the **Bubba Gump Shrimp Co. Restaurant** (Pier 39, tel. 415/781–4867), based on the film *Forest Gump*, has it. Also see Alcatraz Island and Pier 39.

**KEEP IN MIND** While UnderWater World can be enjoyable and educational, a family of four could easily spend $1 a minute or more for the experience. Factor in the well-stocked gift shop, which you enter when you "resurface." Loaded with undersea-related merchandise ranging from books and jewelry to sweatshirts and stuffed sharks, it's bound to catch your kids' eyes. (Just try to get out without some shark or other taking a bite out of your wallet.) And that's not counting all the other ways to blow your budget on Pier 39. So consider the cost before taking the plunge.

 Beach St. at the Embarcadero

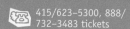 415/623-5300, 888/
732-3483 tickets

 $12.95 ages 12 and up, $6.50
children 3–11; $29.95 families

 Daily 9–8

 3 and up

Narration—provided via headphones—is jaunty and informative, but there's a coordination problem between the length of the tape, which runs about 40 minutes, and the length of time it takes to ride the slow-moving walkways through the tunnels—only 20 to 30 minutes. Those people who reach the end of their "dive" in just ½ hour or so will miss some of the taped descriptions, so to get your money's worth, from time to time you really need to get off the moving walkway onto a parallel stationary platform and stroll at your own pace or linger for a spell. You should also be aware that it's a bit awkward taking strollers on the moving walkway, and kids need to be age 6 or so to appreciate the headphone narration, though young children can certainly admire all those fish.

We can only wonder whether the fish, without benefit of headphones, can admire all those humans moving past inside their "tank."

**HEY, KIDS!** When you're traveling through the tunnels at Under-Water World, see how many different species of sharks you can count—you might see as many as seven. Watch for leopard sharks (they have spots), spiny dogfish sharks (they're long and thin), six gill sharks (count the gills), seven gill sharks (add one more gill), plus smoothhound, Pacific angel, and soupfin sharks—what, you think you're going to get clues for all of them?

# UNION SQUARE

This square at the heart of San Francisco is a bustling place. Cable cars clang as they rumble past the landmark Westin St. Francis Hotel. Department stores buzz with shoppers. Area theaters draw packed houses to Broadway-style plays and musicals, and special events often draw crowds.

The park in the center of the square is a mix of green grass, palm trees, and concrete, with benches that are often occupied by "men of leisure." Traditionally, more people have scurried through this crossroads—residents and visitors alike heading from Market Street to Chinatown or from the Financial District to the Theater District—than have stopped to pull up a seat on a bench or stretch out on the grass. But that may change when a long-talked-about renovation takes place in the next few years.

Union Square is certainly *the* mecca for shoppers in San Francisco, and many of the city's finest and ritziest stores are on or right around it. But there's plenty here for families to buy,

KEEP IN MIND The main cable car turnaround is just down Powell Street (at Market Street). Although there's often a long line there, you don't have to wait in it. It's perfectly acceptable to hop on a car when it stops at Union Square, though you probably won't get a seat that way. However, if the car is filled to overflowing, it may not be safe to try hopping on with small kids.

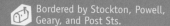 Bordered by Stockton, Powell, Geary, and Post Sts.

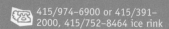 415/974-6900 or 415/391-2000, 415/752-8464 ice rink

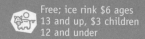 Free; ice rink $6 ages 13 and up, $3 children 12 and under

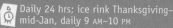 Daily 24 hrs; ice rink Thanksgiving–mid-Jan, daily 9 AM–10 PM

 5 and up

too. Some of the main draws are the Disney Store (400 Post St.), Sanrio (39 Stockton St.), F.A.O. Schwarz (48 Stockton St.), and Niketown (278 Post St.). Just about two blocks from the square, down at Market Street, there's a Virgin Megastore (2 Stockton St.) and, across the street from that, the sparkling San Francisco Shopping Centre (865 Market St.), containing a Warner Bros. Studio Store and a dizzying nine-story atrium with spiral escalators that most kids can't resist riding.

In winter, the Westin St. Francis Ice Rink sets up on Union Square, a magical setting amid the holiday lights and decorated windows of surrounding department stores.

While you're downtown, if you need information about San Francisco, stop by the San Francisco Visitors Bureau office at Hallidie Plaza (Market and Powell Sts.). Or just sit in the park and soak up local color.

**KID-FRIENDLY EATS** **Planet Hollywood** (2 Stockton St., tel. 415/421-7827) is overpriced, but kids eat up the memorabilia. Popular **Sears Fine Foods** (439 Powell St., tel. 415/986-1160), known for its little pancakes, is closed for dinner. The **Compass Rose** (Westin St. Francis, tel. 415/397-7000) serves afternoon tea (or cocoa) as well as lunch.

**HEY, KIDS!** If you and your parents stop in to see the famous Westin St. Francis Hotel (335 Powell St., tel. 415/397-7000), be sure to take a ride on one of the outdoor glass elevators. They're some of the fastest elevators in the city, and they'll whisk you to the top of the hotel while yielding views of downtown, the Bay Bridge, and Coit Tower along the way.

# WELLS FARGO HISTORY MUSEUM

A museum off a bank lobby? A bit unusual, but nevertheless well worth seeking out when you're downtown. Wells Fargo began banking and express operations in San Francisco in 1852, just after the Gold Rush of 1849 lured thousands of treasure-seekers to California. The company delivered letters, safeguarded money and valuables, and bought, sold, and transported gold.

In 1861, the company ran the fabled Pony Express between Sacramento and Salt Lake City as part of the Pony Express's 10-day mail-delivery service between San Francisco and Missouri (the same time it takes today, it sometimes seems). The cost was 10¢ per ½ ounce (as opposed to 3¢ for a letter through the U.S. mail). By the late 1860s, Wells Fargo stagecoaches dominated overland mail and transportation in the West. So although the museum is in part a commercial for the West's oldest bank, it also documents a colorful slice of California history.

**KID-FRIENDLY EATS** *See* China-town and Embarcadero Center for information on nearby eateries.

**HEY, KIDS!** Don't miss the old telegraph machine in a corner of the first floor. Here you can send messages back and forth between two tables via Morse Code, just the way Wells Fargo agents did in the 19th century. (There's a Morse Code chart there to help out.) . -. .— — -.— .-.-.- (Translation: *Enjoy.*)

420 Montgomery St.

 Free

 415/396-2619

M–F 9–5

6 and up

Nicely presented exhibits cover two floors. As you enter, you'll see the 1867 Wells Fargo and Company Overland Stage Coach, one of 10 passenger coaches used in the company's Great Overland Mail Route from the Bay Area to St. Louis. Payment got each of nine tightly packed passengers a "through-ticket and 15 inches of seat." Nearby, you'll find a re-created early-day Wells Fargo office—complete with telegraph, agent's desk, documents, treasure boxes, and package scales. Other exhibits focus on stagecoach drivers, the bandit-poet known as Black Bart, the Pony Express, and the Gold Rush, comprising collections of gold samples, mining tools, and other mementos of the era. On the second floor, your kids can climb on a cutaway stagecoach seat, take the reins, and play driver. Nearby sits a coach (without wheels) that the entire family can squeeze into to get a feel for just how cramped— and no doubt hot and sticky—it got inside. There's also a first-floor general store where you can pick up souvenirs, such as gold-panning kits and model stagecoaches. The only thing you can't do is send a letter for 10¢.

KEEP IN MIND Though the museum's Financial District location isn't exactly a family mecca, it's an easy walk from such areas as Chinatown and the Embarcadero (see above), so you might want to combine a visit here with some sightseeing there. The museum is also just a short walk from the California Street cable car line.

# WINCHESTER MYSTERY HOUSE

Sarah Winchester's 160-room Victorian dwelling is touted as the "world's oddest historical mansion," and it's certainly a top contender for that honor. A wealthy widow—she was heiress to the Winchester rifle fortune—and devotee of the occult, Winchester began work on her house in 1884. After her husband and baby daughter died, Winchester apparently was convinced by a spiritualist that continuous building would appease the spirits of those killed by Winchester firearms and win eternal life for herself. That plan failed—she eventually died at age 82—but it certainly kept a platoon of carpenters employed. Following no discernible blueprints, they worked on the mansion 24 hours a day for the next 38 years (ending with her death in 1922).

The results are both beautiful and bizarre: Rooms with Tiffany art-glass windows, gold and silver chandeliers, inlaid doors, and parquet floors are juxtaposed with stairways and chimneys that lead nowhere, doors that open to blank walls, windows that are built into floors, and a layout so rambling and complex that the guides quip, "If you get separated from the group,

**KEEP IN MIND** Very young kids could get restless during the hour-long tour, and that presents some problems: Since you aren't allowed to wander on your own—you'd get lost—there's no way to bail out. But for school-age kids and up, the tour is surprisingly interesting. The narration isn't confined to stuffy descriptions of house and family; it's jaunty and, like the tour itself, covers a lot of ground. Also note that strollers can't be accommodated. There are simply too many stairways and narrow passages.

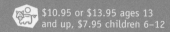

there's no guarantee you'll ever be found." Even Winchester and her servants used maps to get around the bewildering maze.

The standard tour lasts one hour and goes through 110 rooms; it's a 1½-mile jaunt in which you'll see many of the house's 40 bedrooms, 47 fireplaces, 17 chimneys, 52 skylights, and six kitchens. A 55-minute behind-the-scenes tour, added in 1998, reveals the previously unseen workings of the estate and is good for return visitors; the downside for families is that elementary school kids aren't allowed on the tour for safety reasons (you have to wear hard hats, too). You can also take self-guided tours of the extensive Victorian gardens and firearms museum, devoted mainly to the Winchester rifle, the "gun that won the West."

## KID-FRIENDLY EATS Winchester Café,

within the Winchester Mystery House, serves snacks, desserts, and drinks, and is a good place to relax after the tour. For good Mexican food, including excellent fajitas with fresh tortillas, as well as special kids' menus, check out the local branch of **Chevys** (550 S. Winchester Blvd., tel. 408/241–0158), just down the street.

**HEY, KIDS!** The Mystery House is a good place to come during Halloween season. You can go trick-or-treating in the gardens here on three nights or take a special flashlight tour of the house after dark. Spooky! The house is also open for evening flashlight tours every Friday the 13th. But check with Mom or Dad first so your spirits aren't dashed. Special night programs run 6 PM–midnight and cost $21 per person; tickets must be bought in advance.

# YERBA BUENA GARDENS

Once a bleak industrial area, the South of Market blocks around—and above—the north and south branches of the Moscone Convention Center have been transformed into a showplace of arts facilities, parks, and entertainment, all called Yerba Buena Gardens. Thanks to recent additions, it's now a premier family playground.

Long talked about and long in the making, the Rooftop at Yerba Buena Gardens, which opened in 1998, occupies 10 acres atop the largely underground Moscone Center South. The Rooftop, reached via a pedestrian bridge over Howard Street from the northern section of Yerba Buena Gardens, is loaded with activities geared to kids, though parents can play, too. A restored 1906-vintage Looff carousel, from the long-defunct Playland-at-the-Beach, is back in action. At the Zeum, a high-tech interactive arts center, kids can create animation or a multimedia video. An NHL-size Ice Skating Center with skyline views is San Francisco's only year-round public rink. Also here are a bowling alley and 3 landscaped acres with a Children's Garden and Play Circle, including a stream, slides, and child-size hedge maze.

**HEY, KIDS!** The city of San Francisco itself was called Yerba Buena from the time it was settled in the late 1700s until 1847. In Spanish, Yerba Buena means "good herb," which probably referred to a type of mint that grew here. When the city began to grow, just before the Gold Rush of 1849, the name was changed to San Francisco, after St. Francis of Assisi. But for many years after the Gold Rush, the city was anything but saintly—it had a wild and rowdy reputation.

 Mission, Howard, or Folsom Sts., between 3rd and 4th Sts.

 415/777-2800 Zeum,
800/638-7366 Metreon,
415/978-2787 arts center

 Free; some attractions charge

 Daily 6 AM–12 AM; attractions, varying hrs

All ages, Zeum 8–18

Opened in 1999, the Metreon, a futuristic Sony Entertainment Center, is adjacent to the parklands above Moscone Center North. It contains an IMAX theater along with 15 regular movie screens, plus an array of shops and restaurants. Three interactive attractions based on literary works will interest families. In the play space inspired by author-artist Maurice Sendak's *Where the Wild Things Are*, children encounter goblins, a hall of mirrors, and a 17-foot-tall Wild Thing. *The Airtight Garage*, based on the work of French graphic novelist Jean "Moebius" Giraud, features a host of electronic and virtual-reality games, including a virtual bowling alley. And in the area based on author-architect David Macauley's *The Way Things Work*, your kids can view a three-screen, three-dimensional show illustrating how mechanical things work—and sometimes don't—with bubbles, smoke, and blasts of air and water. Access to all three costs $17 ages 13 and up, $13 children 3–12.

KID-FRIENDLY EATS **Mo's Gourmet Hamburgers** (adjacent to Zeum, tel. 415/957-3779) is an outpost of a North Beach restaurant. Metreon has several good restaurants. Try **In the Night Kitchen,** an American diner with a Maurice Sendak theme and outdoor seating, or **LongLife Noodle Co.** (tel. 415/369-6188), which serves Asian noodles.

KEEP IN MIND There are two major garden spaces: the Esplanade, above Moscone Center North, and the East Garden, to its east. The Esplanade has well-tended gardens, grass, and a terrace with outdoor cafés. Below the terrace, the Martin Luther King Jr. Memorial Fountain includes a 50-foot-wide, 20-foot-high waterfall children scamper behind.

games

**"I'M THINKING OF AN ANIMAL..."** With older kids you can play 20 Questions: Have your leader think of an animal, vegetable, or mineral (or, alternatively, a person, place, or thing) and let everybody else try to guess what it is. The correct guesser takes over as leader. If no one figures out the secret within 20 questions, the first person goes again. With younger children, limit the guessing to animals and don't put a ceiling on how many questions can be asked. With rivalrous siblings, just take turns being leader. Make the game's theme things you expect to see at your day's destination.

**"I SEE SOMETHING YOU DON'T SEE AND IT IS BLUE."**
Stuck for a way to get your youngsters to settle down in a museum? Sit them down on a bench in the middle of a room and play this vintage favorite. The leader gives just one clue—the color—and everybody guesses away.

# FUN WITH THE ALPHABET

**"I'M GOING TO THE GROCERY..."** The first player begins, "I'm going to the grocery and I'm going to buy... " and finishes the sentence with the name of an object, found in grocery stores, that begins with the letter "A". The second player repeats what the first player has said, and adds the name of another item that starts with "B". The third player repeats everything that has been said so far and adds something that begins with "C" and so on through the alphabet. Anyone who skips or misremembers an item is out (or decide up front that you'll give hints to all who need 'em). You can modify the theme depending on where you're going that day, as "I'm going to X and I'm going to see..."

**"I'M GOING TO ASIA ON AN ANT TO ACT UP."** Working their way through the alphabet, players concoct silly sentences stating where they're going, how they're traveling, and what they'll do.

**FAMILY ARK** Noah had his ark—here's your chance to build your own. It's easy: Just start naming animals and work your way through the alphabet, from antelope to zebra.

**WHAT I SEE, FROM A TO Z** In this game, kids look for objects in alphabetical order—first something whose name begins with "A", next an item whose name begins with "B", and so on. If you're in the car, have children do their spotting through their own window. Whoever gets to Z first wins. Or have each child play to beat his own time. Try this one as you make your way through zoos and museums, too.

# JUMP-START A CONVERSATION

**games**

**wiggles**

**WHAT IF...?** Riding in the car and waiting in a restaurant are great times to get to know your youngsters better. Begin with imaginative questions to prime the pump.

- If you were the tallest man on earth, what would your life be like? The shortest?
- If you had a magic carpet, where would you go? Why? What would you do there?
- If your parents gave you three wishes, what would they be?
- If you were elected president, what changes would you make?
- What animal would you like to be and what would your life be like?
- What's a friend? Who are your best friends? What do you like to do together?
- Describe a day in your life 10 years from now.

**DRUTHERS** How do your kids really feel about things? Just ask. "Would you rather eat worms or hamburgers? Hamburgers or candy?" Choose serious and silly topics—and have fun!

**FAKER, FAKER** Reveal three facts about yourself. The catch: One of the facts is a fake. Have your kids ferret out the fiction. Take turns being the faker. Fakers who stump everyone win.

# KEEP A STRAIGHT FACE

**"HA!"** Work your way around the car. First person says "Ha." Second person says "Ha, ha." Third person says "Ha" three times. And so on. Just try to keep a straight face. Or substitute "Here, kitty, kitty, kitty!"

**WIGGLE & GIGGLE** Give your kids a chance to stick out their tongues at you. Start by making a face, then have the next person imitate you and add a gesture of his own—snapping fingers, winking, clapping, sneezing, or the like. The next person mimics the first two and adds a third gesture, and so on.

**JUNIOR OPERA** During a designated period of time, have your kids sing everything they want to say.

**IGPAY ATINLAY** Proclaim the next 30 minutes Pig Latin time, and everybody has to talk in this fun code. To speak it, move the first consonant of every word to the end of the word and add "ay." "Pig" becomes "igpay," and "Latin" becomes "atinlay." To words that being with a vowel, just add "ay" as a suffix.

# MORE GOOD TIMES

**BUILD A STORY** "Once upon a time there lived..." Finish the sentence and ask the rest of your family, one at a time, to add another sentence or two. Bring a tape recorder along to record the narrative—and you can enjoy your creation again and again.

**NOT THE GOOFY GAME** Have one child name a category. (Some ideas: first names, last names, animals, countries, friends, feelings, foods, hot or cold things, clothing.) Then take turns naming things that fall into that category. You're out if you name something that doesn't belong in the category—or if you can't think of another item to name. When only one person remains, start again. Choose categories depending on where you're going or where you've been—historic topics if you've seen a historic sight, animal topics before or after the zoo, upside-down things if you've been to the circus, and so on. Make the game harder by choosing category items in A-B-C order.

**COLOR OF THE DAY** Choose a color at the beginning of your outing and have your kids be on the lookout for things that are that color, calling out what they've seen when they spot it. If you want to keep score, keep a running list or use a pen to mark points on your kids' hands for every item they spot.

**CLICK** If Cam Jansen, the heroine of a popular series of early-reader books, says "Click" as she looks at something, she can remember every detail of what she sees, like a camera (that's how she got her nickname). Say "Click!" Then give each one of your kids a full minute to study a page of a magazine. After everyone has had a turn, go around the car naming items from the page. Players who can't name an item or who make a mistake are out.

**THE QUIET GAME** Need a good giggle—or a moment of calm to figure out your route? The driver sets a time limit and everybody must be silent. The last person to make a sound wins.

# THEMATIC INDEX

# ACKNOWLEDGMENTS

To my parents, Clark and Mary Norton, with loving thanks, who introduced me to San Francisco when I was age 9. For providing invaluable information, assistance, and suggestions for this book, the author would like to thank Laurie Armstrong; Nick and Esther Baran; Mel, Emily, and Natalie Flores; Mimi Sarkisian; Pat and Anne Forte; Michael and Beth Ward; Michael and Mary Reiter; Veronica Daly; Sheldon Clark; Bob Siegel; Pat Koren; Mary Viviano; Lana Beckett; and my most faithful researchers and travel companions, Catharine, Grael, and Lia Norton.

I'm also grateful to my ever-supportive and instructive editors at Fodor's, including Caroline Haberfeld, Andrea Lehman, and Danny Mangin.

—Clark Norton

the end